Silence
Equals Death

Exposing The Deeds
Of Darkness

Third Printing

Rettie A. Winfield

Silence Equals Death

Exposing The Deeds Of Darkness

Rettie A. Winfield

Please direct all inquiries to:
The Bible Church Of Christ Inc.
100 West 2nd Street
Mt. Vernon, New York 10550

Edited by:
Minister Montrose Bushrod • Minister Andrea Hester

PUBLISHED BY:
BRENTWOOD CHRISTIAN PRESS
4000 BEALLWOOD AVENUE • COLUMBUS, GEORGIA 31904

A MOMENT OF PRAYER:

Dear Heavenly Father, thank you for the courage and knowledge to write this book. I pray that the same Holy Spirit that motivated me to write the words of these pages, will fall upon every reader. Lord, let the power of your anointing permeate every mind, body, soul, and spirit. Let the ultimate goal be accomplished Lord, which is to win souls for your kingdom. All the glory, honor and praise belongs to you, for great is thy faithfulness.

These and all things I pray in the name of Jesus Christ.

Amen.

DEDICATION

With a poem I have dedicated this book to Evangelist Antoinette Cannaday. It is my way of saying thank you through these few words of expression.

EVANGELIST ANTOINETTE CANNADAY

God has adorned you with the glory of angels, heavens light shines upon you illuminating the beauty that meekness has left behind. Humility thanks you for turning your back on pride and arrogance, as victory congratulates you with a kiss as your battles are already won.

Evangelist Cannaday, a woman or a servant? The anointing of God has permeated your very existence causing you to become a life changing experience to all who encounters you. Powerful woman of God, truly you are a vessel unto honor, the Lord has called you forth for such a time as this. Even faith can hear your spirit crying, "Let my people go!" Perhaps that is why boldness proudly waves his banner of victory on your behalf.

Evangelist Cannaday, an author, a teacher, a mentor, a playwright, a street preacher, a mother, a friend. Evangelist Cannaday an exorcist anointed by God!

SPECIAL THANKS:

First and foremost I must start by thanking our Lord and Savior Jesus Christ. For nothing is done without his knowledge and consent.

I would like to thank my sister Sheree Manlove. My sister stood in the gap on my behalf for over seven years. When it seemed as if I would never answer the call that God had on my life, she never gave up on me. It is because of her, I truly know, that the prayers of the righteous availeth much.

I would like to give a special thank you and a hardy God bless you to my 12 brothers and sisters; Stroza, Sheree, Geronamo, Albert, Paul, Karec, Richard, Stephanie, George Jr., Cindy, Ronald, and Regina, I love you all.

A special thanks to my God Mother Ernestine Blount:

Thank you for all the beautiful childhood memories. Having you in my life made the sun in my heart shine brighter, may God continue to bless you.

A VERY SPECIAL
ACKNOWLEDGMENT

I would like to thank my pastor Bishop Roy Bryant Sr., D.D. and his wife Mother Sissieretta Bryant. My loving pastor and his wife have devoted over forty years of their life to the ministry of Jesus Christ. Because of their commitment to the gospel, countless amounts of people have received the baptism of the Holy Spirit with the evidence of speaking in tongues according to acts 2:4. Because of their blessed deliverance and demonology ministry many people including myself have been set free by the power of God. I would like to thank my pastor for the investment that he has made into my life and also for providing me with the opportunity to maximize my God given potential.

Bishop Roy Bryant Sr., D.D. is also the author of "Manual On Demonology - Diary Of An Exorcist" and "Manual On Demonology #2 - Satan The Motivator", as well as one of the world's greatest exorcist who is teaching and working in demonology today.

Bishop Roy Bryant Sr., D.D. and Mother Sissieretta Bryant, thank you for all that you have done for me, and may God continue to richly bless you both.

FROM THE AUTHOR TO YOU

I would like to thank you for selecting this book. I pray that you will find joy in knowing that every word of it is true, however, some of the names have been changed in compliance with the law. Although some readers may find certain issues breath taking and shocking, I am proud to say that all facts stated can be traced back to the Bible. It is my prayer that you will find as much joy in reading this book as I found in writing it.

May God bless you all.

AUTHOR'S PREFACE

I was born in Belhaven, North Carolina on April 5, 1967 to a young couple by the name of George and Gladys Winfield. Due to financial hardships, at three months old my parents gave me to my aunt Mamie and uncle Jacob Hill to be raised in upstate New York. From that moment until now, my uncle and aunt have been my mother and father. However, I am blessed with a beautiful and close relationship with both sets of parents, and I love all four as if they were one.

I would like to take this time to thank both sets of parents, as they have all contributed to who I have become.

May God continue to bless you all.

CONTENTS

9

1

ALL MEN ARE DOGS

"All men are dogs. I hate men! They are worthless, spineless, meaningless occupants of perfectly good space. If I had it my way, the earth would be void of men altogether, except for my brothers, of course. Knowing them, I'm sure they wouldn't mind a setup like that. If I thought I could get away with it, I would kill them all off myself. Yes, I'll kill him so he can never hurt me or anyone else again. My parents think our next door neighbor is so great, they kiss the ground he walks on, outright worships him if you ask me. They tell him everything that goes on in our home and that's why I'm so vulnerable. Can't anyone see that I'm hurting, scared, angry, and flat out vexed?

I hate being in this "black box." Someone let me out! Mom, Dad, can't you stop him? He's your friend. I guess you can't stop what you refuse to face. Fine, when I grow-up, you'll never hold a grandchild that came from my womb. I'll see to it that you never get to see me walk down the aisle. Do you know why? Because I will never let another man touch me again, much less get close enough to marry me.

When I grow-up, if I ever see that black snake who keeps touching me, I will kill him right in the very tracks where he slithers. Who could be so cruel? God, are you there? If anyone can stop this, You can. God, can you hear me? Can anyone hear me?"

All these thoughts ran through my head as a 180 lb. 40 "something" year-old man was writhing on top of my 7 year-old body in the back seat of his car. He would always tell me, "If anyone finds us and they ask what is going on, you tell them you're sick and I'm trying to help you. Do you understand?" I understood all right. I understood that I'm not the one who is sick.

After each incident, which went on for a period of about six years or so, he would almost always buy me something or give me money. Once he bought me a music box with a little ballerina that spun around as the music played. Little did I know how symbolic it was to the life which lay before me, stagnant, boxed in, and turning around in circles.

How degrading it is to give a little girl money for sex. I felt like a childhood whore, plus, I felt so alone. I tried to tell my father more times than I could count, but every time I opened my mouth, nothing would come out. I mean I tried, and I tried, and I tried but when I say nothing would come out, that's just what I mean!

The older I got, the more bitter I became. Hate was my best friend and it began to bring me comfort, so I thought. It's the only emotion I knew deep down inside and it was my only defense. I thought that hate would keep me safe from the dragon next door. I had enough anger and hate in my heart that if it were at all possible I would have snatched that man's soul from his rib cage and catapulted his spirit into the jaws of a rotten rattlesnake. "Swallow him whole!", I would scream. and pray that the snake's belly was the pit of hell.

I remember the times that he would ask my mother if I could come over and clean his house for him. His wife worked days so it was convenient for him to have children over at that time.

One day as I was cleaning his wife's room (he and his wife slept in separate bedrooms) I heard him call me by my nickname, "Rita." As I turned to respond to his call, there he was standing outside of the doorway masturbating. I had never seen a grown man's body before and it practically scared me to death. I let out a scream and ran for the stairs. Three of my little footsteps equaled one of his, so catching me was not a problem. He grabbed me from behind by my arm, and put his hand over my mouth. The fear that I felt at that moment can never be described. The last thing that I remember was the tears that rolled down my face, over his hand, and down to the floor. After that, I blacked out and even to this day, can't remember a thing.

Even after that day my mother continued to send me over to his house, but I had never told her what was happening because I was just too mortified. To add insult to injury, I didn't think that she would believe me. The flip side to the scenario was that if she did believe me, there was a good chance that she would have tried to kill him, that is if my father didn't beat her to it. Consequently my options were looking more and more grim with each passing day.

Once again I had found myself in the dragon's den. As time went on, he became more and more confident that I wouldn't tell anyone, so the stakes got higher.

Soon he began to introduce me to pornographic books that he kept in his spare room upstairs.

He would perform masturbation on me and force me to return the favor. He would take pictures of me and engage in hours of sexually perverted conversations. One day I asked him, "Why are you doing this? You have a daughter, how would you feel if someone was doing this to her?" He responded by saying "Someone is doing this to my daughter." I asked "Who." He said, "Your father. See, your father and I have a deal, we decided that we would get you girls ready for life by showing you how things are done. Your father gave me permission to do this."

Even then I knew he was lying. His daughter lived in Florida and we lived in New York. We only saw his daughter once every eight years or so, not to mention the fact that she was many years older than me, and she already had a young son.

The web that this man spun was deep and wide. He was a trusted man in our community partly because he worked in the justice field. He had access to guns because he worked in the prisons, counseling I think.

He would often use his guns as a scare tactic when he would rape me from time to time. I don't ever recall him pointing them at me or anything, he would just leave them on the night table or dresser and bring up conversations about them. To me that was threatening enough.

As I got older quite naturally I got wiser. I was no longer afraid to fight back. The first time I can recall fighting back was a day that I was standing near the fireplace in his living room. I was fascinated with a box of self-starting matches that he kept on top of the mantel. As I looked at the matches he walked up behind me and began to force himself on me. I picked up one of the long stemmed wooden matches and struck it against the bricks of the fireplace. I took the flaming match and stuck it into his hand. I'll never forget the way his skin sizzled as the smoke seemed to come out of his fingertips. He pushed me away and let out an evil scream. He was so mad that his face turned three shades darker. I ran as fast as I could into the bathroom which was strangely located in the kitchen. He followed me to the bathroom and tried to open the door, he couldn't because it was locked. "Come out, I won't hurt you. Come out I said!" Like I was really going to trust someone who just tried to rape me. I don't remember how long I stayed in the bathroom that day, but it was the beginning of a "life time" of fighting back.

I can even remember times when I wasn't even safe in my own home from this man. I can recall all to well an early autumn morning, I was asleep in my bedroom. I felt someone's hands pawing all over my body. Then I felt someone's face getting close to mine, he was trying to kiss me. I was so afraid and confused. I couldn't understand why this was happening to me in my own house, in my own room! I opened my eyes and saw this huge dark silhouette against the canopy on my bed. I began to fight back, I scratched his face and I just began swinging. It was at that moment I heard my father's voice calling for his best friend as he stood at the bottom of the staircase. "I'm going to miss my plane." Then he walked quickly and quietly out of my room and down the steps to take my father to the airport.

To this day I don't know why I didn't scream. I can only compare it to a person who sees an on coming train and doesn't move out of the way. Fear can be one of life's most paralyzing forces.

After that morning I almost never had a peaceful nights sleep in my bedroom again. I would often get a visitation from this "thing", an evil presence that would try to convince me that it was the Holy Spirit. What was even more strange was the fact that I didn't really know what or who the Holy Spirit was. I was almost always in constant fear and torment. At night the evil force would enter into my room, and bring me to a shallow level of consciousness. I could look all around my room and I could even see my family as they walked around in the hallway, but I couldn't move. I would hear this loud over bearing siren sound in my ears. Then I would feel something like worms squirming all through my body, it was hellish and sad.

My grades dropped in school, at one point in elementary school I was a straight "F" student. I had no span of attention and I was tired all the time because I wasn't getting enough sleep. To say that I was a bright child was an understatement, I was a brilliant child with creative skills that went through the roof. Yet all was hindered by the mental concentration camp that I lived in for so many years. I would think to myself, if only I could scream, maybe someone would hear me and come to my rescue.

As I approached my adolescent stage, I didn't think it was humanly possible to dislike men any more than I did. Needless to say at that point having a boy friend was not even an option for me. However, I began to desire relationships on a more intense level than "just friends." I was perplexed at the fact that a lot of my teen-aged girl friends had begun to find me attractive. Not knowing what "gay or homosexual" was or even meant, I immediately attributed the attraction to the fact that I was very athletic and quite a tomboy. Little did I know that a much greater force was at play.

These young girls began writing me love letters and calling my house at all times of the night and day. On an average school day, I would receive approximately fifteen calls before dinner. Sometimes the older sisters of my peers would call me also. I sincerely didn't know what was happening to me. At first I was afraid, but then I began to like all of the attention. I stored all of my love letters in an old shoe box, I would read them over and over again. At first I didn't understand all of the explicit requests in the letters, but it didn't take long before I learned the ropes and inevitably relationships began to ignite. For the first time in my life I was able to have an intimate relationship with another human being and not feel threatened or overtaken. I thought that this was the greatest discovery and breakthrough of my life.

I began to find the comfort that I so desperately needed within my new relationships. I felt as if I could tell my girlfriends most anything since they were the total opposite of everything that I learned to hate. Little did I know, I was getting in way over my head.

Although I had a new focal point and the molestation and rapes had stopped; the visitations, the nightmares, the fears, the torment, and the hate did not. I was an emotional shipwreck inside, and no one knew it except me and God.

By the time I was 15 years old the torment had become unbearable and I knew I had to find help. I had heard of a group affiliated with the church that me and my siblings attended when we were younger. The name of the Christian group was "The Light House", the group was a small team of young adults who supported teenagers with Godly counsel, fellowship and love.

I was told by one of the ladies that my mother baby-sat for that the Light House convened every Wednesday at 7:00 p.m. Her words were music to my ears. Finally help was on the way. Needless to say I anxiously awaited the night of the next meeting.

Finally Wednesday night came, I walked down the block to the meeting. I couldn't help but wonder who would be there and what were they like. I knocked on the door and I was greeted by a very friendly face. "God bless you. Come in." Everyone was so warm and friendly. Someone was playing the guitar, someone else played the piano, while everyone sang and praised God. The smell of freshly baked bread and cookies filled the quaint and cozy living room. The presence of God was there in a way that I had never known. At the end of the program, I approached the leader of the teen group. She was a very nice and friendly, "thirty something" year old with an anointing that was a direct gift from God. I asked her if I could speak with her alone. She took me into another room, a very big room I might add, with tall windows and white curtains. She looked me straight in the eyes and asked me 'what was wrong'. It seemed as if our eyes locked together forever before I could get even one word out. Tears started to flow down my face like a river, to my surprise words began to surface. I could only get four little words to come out of my mouth, just four. All I could say through the river of tears was, "I don't like boys." Immediately, she knew just what I was trying to tell her. She asked if she could pray with me and needless to say, I agreed.

We sat on the sofa in this beautiful seventeenth century house, and she began to pray. She began speaking in a language that I had never heard. I felt something fall upon me so soft and gracefully. I began to fall over as if I was going to sleep but I was wide-awake. I didn't understand it all then, but I had just received the baptism of the Holy Spirit. In the spirit, I saw something similar to gloomy saran wrap over my eyes. As she kept praying, the saran wrap began to burn off of my eyes and I could "see" like I could never see before. In an instant I began to understand spiritual concepts. I also had something similar to an out of body experience. Although I was clearly slumped over on the sofa (under the anointing) somehow at the same time I was across the room looking back at us. It was then that I saw approximately seven demons leave my body, exiting from my back, and leave the room by way of the tall window behind us. In the spirit I heard these demons tell me, "We'll be back, we'll bring others and we'll be stronger." Although what these spirits told me was completely Biblical (under certain circumstances / read Luke 11:24-26) at this point I had virtually no exposure or knowledge of the Word of God. It was that night that I received the baptism of the Holy Spirit and accepted the Lord Jesus Christ as my personal Lord and Savior.

For a while I continued to go to the Light House. I began to go to church with the lady who prayed for me and we became very close friends. My mother however, didn't know this lady and she didn't know what kind of church it was that she was taking me to. For all she knew it could have been an occult.

Out of fear and lack of understanding, my mother forbade me to see her anymore and cut off our friendship. I was devastated, this lady was the first positive and Godly influence that I ever had in my life. She was my first exposure to the anointing and God used her to teach me so much about who He was and what His Word really meant. However, she respected my mothers wishes and stayed away. As time past I lost total contact with her. The last I heard, she had moved to South Africa to preach the Gospel and that she had gotten married to a man she met there. To this day I do not know were she is. It hurts me that she may never know the impact that she had on my life.

After experiencing the lost of my first true friend, I was more angry and bitter than ever. Although I loved my parents with all of my heart, I had become very angry with them. I felt as if they were under some kind of spell or something. Everyone I shouldn't have been with, they allowed me to be with them. Everyone I should have been with, they kept me from them. All of these childhood disappointments set me up for an eleven-year sin spree that almost ended in death on numerous occasions.

By the time I started High School, I had began lying my way out of the house, and sneaking into gay bars and night clubs. At this point meeting other people with the same interest was a breeze. I began making "so called" friends and developing a whole new support system. These "so called" friends tried to introduce me to a little bit of everything under the sun, including drugs. Fortunately I've never been interested in drugs, the most I had ever tried once or twice was marijuana.

What hurts the most as I look back on these times is the fact that all those women knew that I was just sixteen or seventeen years old, and not one of them ever tried to persuade me to change my direction. They all just kept encouraging me to come into "the life."

Older women would come to my high school to pick me up and take me away to be a part of their little sexual fantasies. I remember one woman in particular who would give me the keys to her house. I would take the school bus to her house, wait for her to come home from work and engage in ungodly activities for hours. In the early 90's I read in the newspaper that this same woman was murdered. She was shot in the head and chest execution style. I pray that in her last seconds on earth, that she "got it right" with God.

On my eighteenth birthday I found myself in bed with yet another older lady. She introduced me to things that I didn't even know existed. My fast life style, drunken sprees and all night excursions began to take its toll on my body. Later that day I had become very ill and was placed in the hospital for over two weeks. It was discovered that I had a rare kidney disease, only myself and one other little boy in all of New York had this condition.

Being in the hospital gave me a lot of time to think. I thought about my friends and what I was doing to my body and how stressed out I was. But even in my deepest despair, I couldn't stop!

After being saved a few years earlier, I knew the difference between right and wrong. I knew what God's Word said about gay and lesbian relationships and what he expected of His children. But something else was in control, what I willed not to do, that I did. I began to remember what those spirits told me that night as they fled through that tall window. They kept their word, they came back and brought more spirits, which were stronger than ever.

I even reflected as far back as my childhood days. I remembered one early Sunday morning when my parents were getting breakfast ready for us. My older brother and I were playing a game in our upstairs hallway. I looked up at the back door window located at the end of the hallway. Out of fear I hit my brother quite hard to get his attention. I said with a loud whispering voice, "Look." My brother held his head up and we both stared at this horrible being on the other side of the door. It was a male, approximately seven feet tall, with muscles upon muscles upon muscles. Without a doubt he was the strongest looking creature that I have ever seen to date. The most frightening aspect of this creature however, was the fact that it had the head of a bull. The horns were long and curved forward. This "thing" stood there staring at us as he breathed in and out with deep breaths, he never said a word or moved one of his big muscles. My brother and I ran as fast as we could down to the safety of our parents. We told them what we had seen but they just thought that we were imagining things and served us our breakfast as if nothing unusual had occurred.

The point that I was making to myself was the fact that the enemy had been lusting after me and my family for years, trying to destroy us by any means necessary. He was looking, lurking, yearning and waiting for the perfect time to move in for the kill. Yet in spite of knowing this, I ignored all of the warning signs and continued to live my life according to the desires of my flesh.

No sooner had I left the doors of the hospital, I was back on the club and bar scene. I hit virtually every gay nightclub in New York, both upstate as well as the City. After exhausting all of the clubs in my state, I began to head west to the Pennsylvania area. Pennsylvania's nightlife had a completely different atmosphere. It was far less "artsy", cynical and condescending. It had more of a soulful, rhythmic groove, I was spellbound and completely taken-in by all of its outrageous entertainment. The clubs were filled with drag shows, strippers and lip sync artists. The female impersonators were unbelievable and you couldn't tell them from the real thing. Some of them looked so much like women that even I had accidentally been fooled on more than one occasion, (which was quite embarrassing I must add). The flashing lights, the "house" music, the wonderment, and the beautiful women were all a part of my new life. I found a world of wealth and money making opportunities in the gay life style and I was going to cash in on it. I had heard Christians say that the world has nothing to offer, but that couldn't be further from the truth. The world has plenty of ungodly enticing things to offer everyone, including money, which is no object to the enemy who desires to steal your soul. I was actually convinced that I had found paradise, unfortunately what I had really found was a modern day Sodom and Gomorra.

I know God wasn't pleased with my rebellion and disobedient choices, yet in spite of myself I could feel Him pulling on my heartstrings. He sent many people to tell me to come back "home" to the arms of His safety. I knew God wanted me to do his will but lining my life up with His Word was just out of the question. I actually felt that if I let God into my heart, He would ruin all of my plans and mess up my life. I began to love and worship my sinful life and I had no desire to change it.

Doors began to open up for me in "the life" as I began to make money doing business on the entertainment circuit. In spite of the torment that flooded my soul I wasn't about to give any of it up.

By the time I was twenty-one years old I was in a destructive live-in relationship that lasted for almost two years. My inner torment had begun to manifest itself as severe anxiety attacks. I was put on tranquilizers when my doctor diagnosed me as having a nervous condition. When I ran out of tranquilizers I would drink Nyquil until I could get my prescription re-filled.

By the age of twenty-two, the nightmares and the torment only got worse. Since the memories of my childhood haunted my mind everyday, I decided that I was going to confront the man who stole my childhood and my peace. After all, why should he have peace after what he had done? But the worst was yet to be told, I later found out that I wasn't alone in this deep pain. He had also raped and destroyed the lives of four other little girls who just so happened to be my sisters! Knowing this, I was more angry and filled with more hate than ever before.

One autumn day I finally set out to confront the dragon. He was outside in his yard raking leaves. I walked up to him. I stood eye to eye with him as I am over six feet tall in my shoes. I had no fear, just hate, yet the fear that I saw in his eyes was as clear as a bell. He started to sweat because he knew that "the day" had come.

I asked him, why did you do the things that you did to me when I was a child? The molestations, the torment, why?

Suddenly the dragon was overtaken with a severe case of amnesia, he couldn't seem to remember a thing! He said "I don't know what you're talking about. I never did those things, I never touched you!" At that point I lost "it" and began to yell and scream. I cursed this man out, for what felt like a half-hour, but since I had lost all sense of time, it could have only been forty seconds. To add insult to injury he had the nerve to begin to insult me! But that didn't stop me. I screamed, "If you never touched me, then how is it that I know that you're not circumcised?" He paused for a moment but then continued to lie and insult me. Suddenly, I hit him in his chest so hard it knocked him back a couple of feet. I was hoping with all of my might that he would hit me back. My plan was to fall to the ground and act like I was almost dead until the ambulance arrived. I intended to press charges and have him arrested, (all after beating him down like a common street dog I might add).

It was the sheer grace of God that I didn't kill him that day. The day may very well had ended in murder if he hadn't ran inside of his house like the sissy that he was.

Fortunately for him, he didn't fall for my ambulance scam, but I did have the pleasure of hitting the only person in this whole world that I hated. After this big explosion, I figured what better time to tell my parents all the things that had happened to me at the hands of their best friend. I had decided that no matter how much it hurt, they had to know.

Right after I left the dragon's yard I drove to my house which was about twenty minutes away. As soon as I arrived, I picked up my phone and called my parents, only to receive the shock of my life. The dragon had beat me to the punch, he called my parents before I could get home. He told them that I had walked into his yard, cursed him out and maliciously attacked him for no apparent reason. If that were not enough, he piled on a host of other lies as well.

After digging through all of the current lies that the dragon had just told my parents, I began laying down the foundation of truth. One of the hardest things that I had to do in my life was to tell my parents in detail what had happened to me. I didn't tell them everything that day, just what I thought that they could handle.

I took my parents on a partial childhood journey which was filled with horror, pain and fears. I told them how my God given childhood innocence was taken from me and how I had been treated like a street whore. I also conveyed to them how my whole life was affected because of it.

My father listened with silence and great sorrow. He couldn't believe that all of this had happened to us, right under his nose. The hurt that he felt that day seemed to reverberate through the phone, and across my soul.

The next day my sister Sheree and I met with our parents, and our father drilled us for further details. As the days went on my father's anger turned into hurt. He was very upset at the fact that my sisters and I never told him what had happened while it was happening. He asked us, "Why didn't you tell us, I always thought we were closer than this." For weeks this was all my father would talk about. Whenever we would spend time together, inevitably the conversation would always land back on the dragon. Over and over again he would ask the same questions, trying to get an understanding, I guess.

As the weeks turned into months, I believe that the pressure became too great for my parents to handle. All of the pain, hurt and self-blame simply caved them in. It truly seemed as if they made some kind of an ancient secret pact with one another, as if Satan himself simultaneously crossed them over the threshold of reality and into the land of delusion and denial.

I don't think it would have been as hard for us if just one of them had fallen into the bowels of denial, but both of them? That was just too much for us to handle. They literally blocked out everything that we told them and resumed their friendship with their best friend, the dragon.

We watched as our parents laughed, talked and fellowshipped with the dragon as if all was well. They never once informed him that we had told them what had happened to us. I once recall my father saying, "I don't really know what happened to you girls, after all I wasn't there." It was comments like those that felt like salt to a wound.

No one but God could have known how painful it was to watch my parents carry on that way. Truly this hurt me more than the years of molestation itself. However, it was the love and commitment that my parents showed in all other areas of my life that helped hold me together.

To stay strong I would think of the good times that my mother and I shared together, just the two of us. When I was a child, every morning my mother would cook us breakfast. After sending my brothers and sister off to school we would prepare for our daily walk downtown. Mom would dress me up in one of the beautiful dresses that she hand-made on her old Singer sewing machine. She loved to sew, so she would always make matching outfits for me and my sister.

After getting all dressed up, off we would go downtown. First stop, Woolworth's for material to make new dresses, then down the street for a day of window-shopping.

"Look mom, the fountain!" I loved the fountain that sat in the center of our town. When the water would shoot high up into the sky, I could see tiny rainbows against the noonday sun. Mom would always give me pennies to pitch into it, "Make a wish" she would say. I would close my eyes just like her. Although I was too small to know what a wish was, it didn't stop me from throwing my pennies.

While pushing my stroller, mom would walk from one end of Main Street to the other, I think it was her way of getting her exercise. Our last stop, the bakery. Mom would always stop there to pick up a snack or some fresh dinner rolls. "A happy face please" I would say to the man behind the counter. I loved the soft cookies that had frosting and a happy face on top.

After returning home we would browse through the Macy's catalog and point out all of the things that we wanted. I had a love for diamond rings. My mother would cut the rings out of the catalog, push holes threw the paper and put the rings on my fingers. "Look at my beautiful rings", I would say, I felt like the prettiest girl in the world. I would walk through the living room showing off my rings to all the doll babies that joined us for snack.

The highlight of my day was when my sister Sheree would come home from school, she always had great stories to tell me about her day. She was the only sister that I grew-up with as a very young child. My other sisters lived in North Carolina, but they always came to visit us during the summer. Because we were the only girls, we shared a special closeness and a bond that has never been broken.

As the smell of a good home cooked meal filled the house, I would hear the clinking sounds of my dad's work boots at the back door. I would run as fast as I could to greet him with a flying leap off of the top step, right into his arms. I could always look forward to a great big hug and kiss from my dad. He would almost always have an arm full of flowers or a hanging plant for mom to add to her indoor jungle.

As for my brothers, I truly thought that they were the strongest boys in the world. They would always impress me with their muscles and give me piggyback rides all throughout the house. My bedroom was located in the front of the house on the third floor of our four story brick home. I loved to look out of my window and watch my brothers as they worked. They had to shovel snow, rake leafs, stack firewood, and weed the garden along with what ever else needed to be done around the house. I must say that my parents made men out of them. Working around the house helped to get us ready for the world and I can proudly say that success has been no stranger to any of us.

Winter bought more than just work to our home, it bought the joy of Christmas. I loved Christmas, it was my most favorite time of the year. Mom and Dad would stop at nothing to see that we had the best Christmas possible. Mom would cook enough food to feed an army; coconut cakes, sweet potato pies, German chocolate cake, collard greens, corn bread, smoked turkey, and the list went on.

Our parents would buy us so many gifts that there was almost no place to walk in our living room. Dolls, trucks, Rockm'-Sockm' Robot's, Evil Kinvel's, G.I. Joe's, Easy Bake Oven's, and board games would flow from the Christmas tree, out of the living room and down the hall.

One year I remember getting a box of Mexican jumping beans, I still can't figure out what made those things jump.

Undoubtedly, these were the seeds that were sown into my soul that kept me alive during the winter storms of my life. Looking back on these times however, made it even the more difficult to understand my parents, how could they be so blind?

It almost felt as if my dad was a different person, a total stranger from the man that I grew to love. Of course I loved my dad, how could I not after all the great times we shared together?

I'll never forget the day that he taught me how to ride my bicycle. We took a short walk to the schoolyard at the end of the block. I was so excited, my bike was as shiny and new as the sparkles in my eyes. It was purple with purple and white plastic strings that hung from the handlebars. I still remember the conversation we had as if it were yesterday. Dad said to me, "Are we going to take those training wheels off today?"

I answered, "Yes Daddy, I'm ready to ride all by myself."

Dad leaned over and unscrewed the training wheels from my bike. This was going to be one of the most exciting days of my life, no training wheels! I knew that my older sister and big brothers would be so proud of me.

Dad said, "Okay Rita, I'm going to hold onto the back of your bike, you keep peddling, I'll be right behind you."

I replied, "Okay Daddy, I'll keep peddling."

I was a little afraid to ride my bike without training wheels, but daddy said that he would be right behind me. I knew if I could count on anyone, I could count on my daddy. I felt safe because he would never let anything happen to me.

I got on my bike as my dad held it steady, and I started to peddle. I kept looking back to make sure that my dad hadn't left me, he was right there, running behind me. As my confidence grew, I started to peddle faster, the cool wind felt soothing as it swept across my face. I could hear my dads voice in the background, "I gotcha, I gotcha, keep peddling, I gotcha."

I had a grin on my face as big as a Cheshire cat. I was doing it! With the help of my daddy I was riding my bike! As I approached the end of the sidewalk, I looked behind me to seek my father's approval. "Boy", did I get the surprise of my life. My dad was way down on the other end of the block, standing there shouting "I gotcha, I gotcha."

The moment I realized that my father was no longer supporting me, I immediately fell flat on my face. "SMASH", It felt as if the whole neighborhood heard me and my bike as we hit the hard concrete.

My Dad ran to my aid. "Are you okay?" After clearing the stars from my head I said "Yes Dad, I'm okay." He encouraged me by saying "See, you did it, all by yourself! Come on, let's try again."

How could I forget such classic moments? "Those were the days." I just wish my father had been there for me when I took the biggest fall of my life. All I ever wanted from my parents was their loyalty and support in my darkest hours.

2

THE STREETS OF PHILADELPHIA

Emotionally I was still lying in the back seat of the dragon's car. I had spent a great deal of my life seeking justice for that little girl who still lived deep down inside of me. As time moved on, it had become more clear to me that there would be no justice. The only thing left for me to do was to move on.

Moving on for me was made a little bit easier because for the first time in my life, I had meet the person of my dreams and I had fallen in love. Her name was China, an odd name considering the fact that she was half African American and half-Greek. She was the most beautiful woman that I had ever seen in my life, she was tall with wavy jet-black hair and deep dark eyes. She was as shapely as an hourglass and as stunning as Neferteri in her black prime.

After a very short courtship, we decided to move in together. Things were going great, after all I loved being in relationships. I had been in relationships before, but this time it was different. For once in my life I was happy and I wanted the world to know it. However, being in a gay relationship was not always easy as self-counsel and self-justification was a must in order to survive.

"Justification" quickly became my best friend and trusted advisor. The thoughts that were conveyed to me by "justification" helped develop my new character, thoughts such as... "Who cares if we're two women, we're not hurting anyone. This is one time I won't keep quiet, I'm proud of who I am. I don't need a man, anyway everyone knows that the best men are women. It takes a woman to do a man's job! I hate men, the only thing a man can do for me is to show me where a woman is. I love taking women from men. I give women the best sex they've ever had, and when I'm finished with them, they'll never want another man again. I like "turning women out", it makes me unexplainably high. I'm a woman, so I know what women like, I know what they want to hear. I don't care if they are married, my energy is strong enough to pull some of the most faithful women away from their men and I know it. There's no need for that any more because now I have my own woman. Just like all of my gay brothers and sisters, I'm "out loud and proud!", silence is no longer a part of my vocabulary. After all, silence equals death. I won't die this time because I'm in control, now I wear the pants. No one is going to take anything away from me again and no man will ever tell me what to do again."

Justification always seemed to have all of the answers, she was strong and powerful. I needed her in my life if I was going to beat all the odds.

Everything in my life was really going great. I was completely happy except for one minor detail, I was sick and tired of living in upstate New York. I wanted a change of pace, I wanted to see and experience other cities. One day I finally mustered up the courage to call China at work and asked her if she would be interested in moving. To my bliss she was very interested.

In less than two weeks after that phone call, we packed up every thing we owned and moved to Philadelphia.

Philadelphia proved to be all that we thought it would be, we hit all the gay clubs and made a few new friends. Life was great as long as I could keep the skeletons in my closet quiet. However, it didn't take long for me to realize that all of my childhood problems had packed up and moved to Philly right along with me.

Unlike my earlier years my pain and frustration showed up in a whole new and gruesome way. Slowly I began to totally dominate China. Although I loved her dearly I was filled with anger, bitterness and hate.

I would go on rampages, throwing and breaking things. At times I would all but completely destroy our house.

As time went on, I had to face the fact that taking my hurts and frustrations out on someone who had nothing to do with my pain was not the answer. Although China had her own problems as well as her own dragons to slay, I must admit that I still deeply regretted all that I put her through.

I had all but completely lost control of my temper as well as my mind, so once again I was put on tranquilizers to control my chronic anxiety and panic attacks. I had begun to go down hill fast and there was nothing that I could do about it.

After three years our relationship grew sour and had become more taxing than ever. Slowly the love that we shared tuned into violence, fear and pain. We tried everything to salvage our relationship, but thank God, nothing worked. In June of our third year together we parted and went on our separate ways.

3

THE FEELINGS ARE REAL

All though homosexuality is wrong, the feelings are very real! Gay people feel all the same hurt and pain that any heterosexual couple feels. Due to social and religious isolation, gay couples tend to become more dependent and/or codependent upon one another. This type of a dysfunctional union can often be detrimental to the persons involved. Unhealthy closeness inevitably leaves the door wide open for the spirit of idolatry to come right in and make himself at home.

Exodus 20:3 clearly states, "Thou shall have no other gods before me." This is the first of the Ten Commandments. To idolize is to worship, whenever you idolize a person place or thing, or even a desire, that idol becomes your god. This includes unnatural affections, if homosexuality is your life style, homosexuality is your god. Believe me when I tell you, there is no God in the homosexual life style, not the true living God.

We as human beings are born into this life with a hole in our existence. The only way to fill this void is to worship. We must worship something, it is as essential as eating and breathing. Even if you traveled to the most remote corners of the world you will find people worshipping something. Who told them to worship? It's just a part of being human.

While yet in my sins I too worshipped a false god and her name was lesbianism. On any given occasion I would have killed or have been killed for my god. I truly had no idea that my relationship had become my religion, until one unforgettable Saturday afternoon.

It was a lazy summer afternoon in Philadelphia. Out of boredom China and I decided to take a stroll down South Street to do a little window-shopping. The smell of pretzels and Philly cheese steaks filled the air with each passing block. As we approached my favorite Italian water ice stand, we couldn't help but notice a small gang of young men up ahead.

As we walked past the men, one of them began making derogatory comments in reference to China's anatomy. He grew angry because she would not respond to his advances. He yelled out, "I know why you wont "give me no play", it's because you're with that dyke!" The more China ignored him, the more angry he became.

The young man had gotten so angry, that he began to run after me. He had plans to "do me in" real bad because China was ignoring him. It wasn't until he came within a few feet of me that he made a few discoveries. One was the fact that I was just as big and as bad as he was. The second discovery was that he was clearly going to get beat down to his last compound in front of his friends. With one look into my eyes he knew that he was in way over his head. What he didn't know was that I had no problem fighting a man over my god, and I had enough abnormal demonic strength to get the job done. I was nothing more than the host of hell encased in a human body. He charged after a "dyke" and found that he had to fight a demon. Thoughts from my old friend "Justification" began to go through my mind, ... "No man is going to threaten me and my woman, who does he think he is, I'll kill him with my bare hands."

This man knew beyond a shadow of a doubt that I was going to beat the living day lights out of him. Getting beat down by a woman in the middle of South Street was just too much for this hoodlum to handle. To my surprise he began to run back towards his friends, but by then it was too late. I wanted a piece of this man and I wanted it bad. In a rage yet in a calm-trance like state, I began to follow him.

Justification had taken over my whole mind, the world was blotted out and the only sound I could hear was her voice.... "He wanted to start trouble, I want to finish it. Who does he think he is? Men don't scare me, I'll fight a man faster than I will a woman." I'm gonna kill this chump, he'll wish that he had never seen a woman." China began to reason with me by saying, "Come on Rettie, it's not worth it, leave that guy alone."

I heard her but I didn't hear her, something else had taken over. I was in a trance of anger and all I wanted was a piece of that man. My eyes were fixed on him, I noticed that he was bending over as he put his hands down into the bushes that lined the street where his friends stood. He pulled out an object, but I couldn't see what it was because it had begun to get a little dark. After getting a handle on the object, he began to approach me, without hesitation I stepped towards him. Out of the shadows he raised his hand. Suddenly, I was staring down the barrel of a 9mm semi-automatic handgun. He raised his hand and aimed the gun at my forehead. This time I looked into his eyes and saw that this young man was wasted on drugs and ready to kill. I froze in my tracks and listened to every hate filled name that he called me. With the gun pointed at my face, I watched as he began to squeeze the trigger.

No more thoughts ran through my head, I felt no fear and I felt no pain. As the trigger pulled tighter, frustration moved across his face. The gun had jammed locked and would not go off. Simultaneously the gunmen and his friends looked to my left as if they had seen a ghost. At that exact moment, they took off running in the opposite direction, never to be seen or heard from again. Without a doubt I believe that they saw something that day, that no one else could see.

After watching the men run away, I can clearly remember walking away and never batting an eye. I never felt fear that day, just anger. I was mostly angry because I didn't get a chance to shred that guy from limb to limb. I was totally oblivious as to what the Lord had just done for me.

The next day I remember thinking, "What was I thinking, how could I have let myself get that angry. I'm out of control! I don't think I can trust my old friend justification any more. Listing to her almost got me killed." Another thought numbed me, had I been killed, I would have surely burst hell wide open. After all I was a backslider and deep down inside I knew that the Lord was trying to get my attention. But I couldn't take heed to the voice of God because I was totally sold out and committed to my fleshly desires. Lesbianism in the form of a relationship had truly become my god.

Had it not been China in that relationship with me, it would have been someone else. The true strong hold was the spirit of lesbianism and in spite of all the warnings I had received from the Lord, I was determined that I was going to live my life my way.

4

THE DEVIL THOUGHT HE HAD ME, BUT I GOT AWAY

After returning to New York, I entered the entertainment business. There were two things I loved most in the world, music and women. Why not combine the both of them and make a living? I began to book myself as a singer and performer in nightclubs and in gay dives. After cutting an under ground single entitled "Is It Love", my engagement calendar really began to pick up.

Everything seemed to be going great, however, I could no longer ignore that feeling of emptiness deep down inside of me. As the months passed, I tried filling the void in my heart with dating and partying. Dating was one of the easiest things for me to do since the ladies loved performers. After a show I would have to beat them off with a stick. I would go home with my pockets filled with telephone numbers, and believe me, I called all of them. Truly the women who passed through my bed and through my life were too many to number, over fifty or sixty I'm sure. Sleeping around helped me keep my pain at bay, it was my way of pretending that everything was great.

But nothing could eliminate the ever present void that lived in my heart.

One night I was alone in my apartment rehearsing for an upcoming gig. I began my usual routine in front my six foot wide mirror. First on the list, turn off all the lights and flick on the night-light. This would give me the same lighting effect as in the nightclubs. Next, get dressed up in the same clothes that I planned on wearing. Most likely a tuxedo jacket or something similar. The lining of my jackets were rigged in order to hold long-stemmed red roses. I would hand them out to all of the ladies during my performances. Last but not least, I would put on the music and begin to rehearse. Although this was something that I did all the time, there was something different about this night, something that I could not explain.

As the mirror and I began our routine, I happened to look myself straight in the eyes. Standing perfectly still, staring at myself, I began to dislike the person who looked back at me. She was tall, dark, smooth and mysteriously inviting. Yet she was lonely, sad, desolate and headed for self-destruction.

It was the void, it had come back to haunt me once again. As desperately as I tried to fill it, nothing worked. At that moment I pulled off my jacket and turned off the music.

I had no idea that I was under the conviction of the Holy Spirit. I knew that the Lord was calling me again, but this night the call was louder and more intense than ever. This time I knew that I had reached the end of the road. I could no longer ignore the calling that was on my life, it was time for a change. After that show date, I never performed again.

Not long after that evening I made it a point to get in touch with a lady named Deb who had been witnessing to me off and on for quite some time. Seeing how much she and her family loved the Lord really made a big impression on my life.

They were attending a local church a few miles outside of our town and she asked me if I would like to visit. I had visited other churches before and I never felt comfortable at any of them. I despised the fact that they were so hung up on clothing. After all I didn't own a dress and I didn't intend to put one on.

Deb's job of getting me to church was made a little bit easier when she told me that her pastor was a woman. A women preacher was far less intimidating, and after all, no man was going to tell me what to do.

The following week, I got dressed up in front of my six-foot wide mirror.

This time I wasn't going to a nightclub I was going to church. In spite of a strange fear and the endless trembling within, I pressed my way to Deb's house and then to church.

As we approached the beautiful historic brick structure in the middle of the block, I could hear the sounds of melodious voices and music lifting up the name of Jesus. The praises were cradled in the wind and swaying in the breeze like brightly colored ribbons. Once in the sanctuary I saw people with their hands lifted towards heaven. They were dancing, singing, jumping and praising God. There were even some people lying on the floor with sheets over them.

Like a fish out of waster, I didn't know what was going on. Talk about culture shock! People were crying and speaking in unknown tongues and I couldn't tell if they were happy or sad. Oddly enough however, with all of these seemingly odd things going on all around me, I was not afraid.

I remember feeling the presence of something that I hadn't felt in a long time, the Holy Ghost. Fire began to burn down on the inside of my soul and the weight of my struggles began to lift off of me.

The time that was spent in praise and worship crushed the hardness of my heart, so by the time the preacher, Bishop Debra E. Gause came forth, I was ready to receive the word of God.

The pastor was a dynamic and anointed speaker. I was amazed to discover how the Lord was using women in ministry. After the sermon, she held a prayer line. There were so many people on the line, I couldn't believe that she was going to pray for each and every one of us.

Soon it was my turn for prayer, she asked me if I was saved. I remember thinking, "Well, I was saved once before as a teenager, some say once saved always saved." My answer to her was, "I don't know." She replied, "If you don't know, you're probably not." At that moment I opened my heart and received Jesus as my personal Lord and savior. She laid hands on me and I was re-filled with the Holy Spirit. The angels are rejoicing I heard someone say as the church began to gave God great glory for my salvation.

I was so happy to be saved, I could see clearly for the first time in my adult life. I was glowing both inside and out because I had the Holy Ghost! What could be better than that? My whole life changed from that moment on.

The devil thought he had me, but I got away!

5

HOMOSEXUALITY THE SPIRIT

I have been anointed and appointed to educate the world and the body of Christ in the area of homosexuality. God is raising up an army in these last days with the courage to speak out against the evil spirit of homosexuality that has plagued our land. Yes homosexuality is a spirit!

Before one can understand the spirit of homosexuality, one must first ask God to open their mind to spiritual principles and truths. A great place to start is with the baptism of the Holy Spirit. The word of God clearly states in Romans 8:9 "But ye are not in the flesh, but in the Spirit, if so be that the Spirit of God dwell in you. **Now if any man have not the Spirit of Christ, he is none of His.**" You must be filled with the Holy Ghost in order to be saved, and in order to have the mind of Jesus. Philippines 2:5 "Let this mind be in you, which was also in Christ Jesus." It is the Holy Spirit that will lead you to the truth, he will open up your mind and your understanding. John 16:13 "Howbeit when he, the Spirit of truth, is come, he will guide you into all truth."

Because human beings are creatures of habit, we tend to do the same things over and over again, often times expecting different results. The definition of this behavior is called, insanity. For ages man has tried to solve spiritual problems with physical, social, and psychological solutions. "News Flash", it doesn't work! Our past has clearly shown us that incarcerating, counseling and sedating demons is not the answer. Remember, these are spirits (Ephesians 6:12). These spirits must be cast out in the name of Jesus in order for a person to truly be free. II Corinthians 10:4 "For the weapons of our warfare are not carnal, but might through God to the pulling down of strong holds." Psychologists and Psychiatrists **do not** have the answers! Jesus never counseled or medicated demons, He cast them out.

Deliverance of this kind does not only apply to the spirit of homosexuality, this applies to all evil spirits. (see examples of other evil spirits listed in the back of this book.)

What is a spirit? The definition of a spirit: 1. A supernatural being, an individual. 2. A disembodied conscious being. 3. The Holy Spirit. 4. An evil force,(i.e. demons).

Contrary to popular belief there are only two main spiritual forces. One is the Spirit of God which is the Holy Spirit and the other is the spirit of Satan which is demonic. Because there is only one true God (who is God all by Himself) there is only the need for one true spirit.

The Holy Spirit was sent to us as our Comforter by Jesus. John 16:7 "Nevertheless I tell you the truth; It is expedient for you that I go away" for if I go not away, the Comforter will not come unto you; but if I depart, I will send him unto you."

There is no shortcomings concerning the Holy Spirit. Through the Holy Spirit, in the name of Jesus all of our needs are met, including healings and deliverance. Our very salvation depends on the Holy Spirit for we must be baptized with the Holy Spirit in order to enter the kingdom of God (Romans 8:9). Make no mistake, water baptism is not the answer to salvation. Mark 1:7-8 "And preached saying, There cometh one mightier than I after me, the latched of whose shoes I am not worthy to stoop down and unloose. 8. I indeed have baptized you with water: but he shall baptize you with the Holy Ghost."

In conjunction with the Holy Spirit angels have been given charge over us. Luke 4:10-11 "For it is written, HE SHALL GIVE HIS ANGELS CHARGE OVER THEE, TO KEEP THEE: AND IN THEIR HANDS THEY SHALL BEAR THEE UP, LEST AT ANY TIME THOU DASH THY FOOT AGAINST A STONE."

The Lord has a flawless system in place to keep his children safe from the wiles of the devil. He covers us with the blood of Jesus which was shed for us on Calvary. He even covers us with armor (Ephesians 6:11) so that we may be able to stand in the evil days.

Satan's spirit however, takes on many diverse and deceptive forms and names. These negative forces are most commonly known as demons. Satan's mission is to kill steal and destroy by any means necessary and he doesn't care how or whom he destroys as long as he is successful.

Believe me when I tell you that Satan does not play fair. His tactics are very subtle, smooth and crafty, yet extremely effective. I once wrote a sermon entitled,

"Imitator of the great Creator." Imitator, that's all the devil is, a big "copycat!" He's not at all creative, he simply perverts and corrupts what God has made Holy. Let's take marriage for example. God created man for woman and woman for man. Our hearts, souls, minds and even our bodies were perfectly designed for one another. As we come together in love, truth and Holy matrimony, the Lord blesses us with the ability to bring forth life (Genesis 9:7).

There is no other form of human reproduction under the sun, nor will there ever be.

Satan however, takes the holiness of matrimony and heterosexuality and perverts them into sinful repulsive acts of homosexuality and fornication. The word of God tells us that the wages of sin is death, (Romans 6:23) His word will never return void. AIDS and sexually motivated crimes kill thousands of people each year. This is just a sample of the multitude of issues that stem from sexual disobedience.

Homosexuality is known to be one of the most enticing and alluring sexual sins ever known to man. Since the days of Sodom and Gomorrah, people have stepped outside of social and religious parameters to indulge in this sin. (The word sodomy was derived from the city of Sodom)

As I began to study demonology, I must say that I was shocked and amazed to learn that there are so many different demonic forces that exist in the spirit realm. Satan's kingdom has an organized system and plan of attack. A demonic spirit never works alone, he always has help from his fellow colleges. For example, even the spirit of homosexuality needs help in order to inhabit and use a person's body. The most common spirit that works along with the spirit of homosexuality is the pedophile spirit. Approximately ninety-five percent of all gays and lesbians have some history of childhood molestation. Approximately seventy-five percent of gays and lesbians have been raped at some point in their lives. (And yes there is a spirit of rape). Spirits don't always wait to use a body to do their dirty deeds. Many people have reported that they have been raped by unseen forces. This rape spirit is known as incubus.

Demonic forces inhabit the bodies of human beings and cause them to commit some of the most heinous crimes known to mankind. Some murders have reported to police that voices told them to murder. The voices that they are hearing are demons and or Satan himself.

The reason that these evil forces are so diverse is because they must appeal to many different types of people around the world. Their objective is to deceive their way into human bodies and or the human spirit. If an evil spirit takes over a person's spirit, that person is officially possessed!

It is extremely important to know that a Holy Spirit filled born again Christian *who is lining-up with the word of God* cannot be possessed. It absolutely cannot happen. However, this same Christian can be oppressed and or have demons living and functioning in different parts of their flesh.

The Apostle Paul wrote in Romans 7:18-20 "For I know that in me (that is, in my flesh) nothing good dwells; for to will is present with me, but how to perform what is good I do not find. 19. For the good that I will to do, I do not do; but the evil I will not to do, that I practice. 20. Now if I do what I will not to do, it is no longer I who do it, but sin that dwells in me."

The Apostle Paul walked in a level of anointing that most people will probably never experience. If a man as great as the Apostle Paul had problems with his flesh, we who are less enlightened can expect the same. Consequently, we must seek deliverance for ourselves.

Many people believe that Christians can not have a demon. Nothing could be further from the truth.

For example, there are many saints who serve and love God with all their hearts. They have been baptized with the Holy Spirit with the evidence of speaking in tongues according to Acts 2:4. Yet some of these same saints can not stop smoking. Because these saint do not want to smoke they have fast and prayed, touched and agreed, yet still they are bound by the spirit of nicotine. Please understand that in no way am I discrediting these methods of prayer, needless to say they do work. However there are times when these spirits need to be cast out. This same principal applies in the homosexual realm. There are many saints of God who still struggle with unnatural feelings years after they have been saved. Some people get deliverance the moment that they receive the Holy Spirit. Other people must seek deliverance at the hands of an exorcist to have the spirit of homosexuality or lesbianism cast out of their body.

It is true however, that God will not dwell in an unclean place. God does not dwell in our flesh (Romans 7:18 "In my flesh dwells no good thing"), it is the flesh that is unclean. We as Christians have a spiritual relationship with God. In John 7:38 Jesus tells us that "He who believes in Me, as the Scripture had said, out of his belly will flow rivers of living water." What is "Living Water"? Living water is the Holy Spirit, it is the anointing of God. Therefore, our belly, (meaning our spirit) is were God lives inside of us. If a person, through disobedience, has had his spirit (belly) taken over by an unclean spirit, he has been possessed. God will not cohabitate in a person's spirit with an unclean spirit. However, if this person is a candidate for deliverance, he can be saved. Once again this is a job for an exorcist. For an even further in-depth study of exorcisms, I strongly suggest the books "Manual On Demonology - Diary Of An exorcist" and "Manual On Demonology #2 - Satan The Motivator" both written by my pastor, Bishop Roy Bryant Sr. D.D. And "Out of Me Went 43 Demons" by Evangelist Antoinette Cannaday.

6

AFTER SHOCK

After rededicating my life to the Lord, the Holy Spirit and I went on an eight-month honeymoon. I sat under the Word of God constantly and I studied and prayed night and day. I ate, slept, and drank the word. It was a whole new world and I was so happy to be a part of it.

To understand my newly found salvation, you must first picture me as a clear bottle of water. The bottom of the bottle was filled with sand, in essence, life was a beach. Soon enough trouble came and the storms of life rocked my bottle back and forth. What was once a beautiful beach became a dirty, messy, ugly, twisted muddy mess. So many unclean things began to fill my heart and my head; unholy soul ties, childhood traumas, unforgiveness, anger, depression, and yes, even lesbianism.

The sandstorms in my life were caused by demons that manifested after I was filled with the Holy Ghost. I thought that all of my problems would be over the moment that I "cried Holy", but instead It seemed to me that they had only just begun. The harder I pressed toward Jesus, the harder things became. I couldn't understand why old feelings were coming back. The results of years of self-destruction had begun to manifest itself, and there was nothing that I could do about it.

Slowly but surely I began to lose my joy. The "after shock" of my salvation was too much for me to handle. I continued to go to church but, with each passing Sunday I would sit further towards the back door. After a while I just stopped going all together.

The flesh was winning, and soon I completely gave into my sexual desires. I had found myself in a flurry of meaningless sexual relationships and before long I was a full fledged backslider living a life of sin.

Yet even in my darkest hour, God never forsook me. The Lord opened my eyes so that I could see into the spirit realm like never before. He allowed me to see some of the spirits who were on assignment to sab otage the ministry that God had planned for me.

One night while sleeping, I was awakened by the movement of someone walking around in my apartment. My eyes opened and I was very much aware of my surroundings, yet I couldn't bring myself to complete consciousness. I could clearly see a man looking through my C.D. tower as if he were going to make a selection. After looking through my C.D.s, he walked over to the sofa that I was sleeping on. It was then that I was able to see his face in full view. He was a jet-black skeleton dressed in a monk type robe with a beaded chain around his waist.

I believe that he had some kind of book hooked onto his side. He put his bony black hands together in a praying position and began to chant over me. At first I thought it was the spirit of death. At that time I had chronic asthma, so quite naturally I thought, "This is the big one!" Before long I realized that this was a mind-binding demon. I believe it was sent to turn my mind reprobate and to put me in a state seven times worse than that which I came.

As I began to gain total consciousness, I quickly sat up on the sofa and as I did, the image that was before me dispersed into the shadows on the floor and walls. At that point I wasn't sure what I should do first, jump out of the window or make a new door as I ran through the wall. All I knew is that I didn't want to be in my apartment if that ugly thing came back.

During that night I recalled how the demon was looking through my music collection. The music that I had did not glorify God and it shouldn't have been in my house. I have always loved music and it was the hardest thing that I ever had to give up. However, when anything unholy is in a person's home, the devil has the right to come in at any time to inspect and or activate his merchandise.

Many nights I would watch spirits walk through my home as if they lived there and they probably did. After all I wasn't living according to the word of God.

True enough sin has its season, howbeit, it is the love of God that is from everlasting to everlasting. After the Lord allowed me to see some of the demons who were after my very soul, I began to seek the Lords face again. By actually seeing into the spirit realm I knew that I couldn't live without Jesus. It's a terrible thing not to have the covering of the Lord in these last and evil days.

Though I had backslid the pull of God never departed from me and before long the Lord renewed my strength, and I began to attend church again.

Although the "after shock" was over, I still had to deal with the reality of my situation. I knew that I was going to have to go back into my past and deal with very bitter and painful issues.

7

"LET'S GET READY TO RUMBLE!"

"Who do you think you are? Take your hands off of my niece. You stole my childhood from me but you won't steal hers." I started to swing, after I punched him in his eye, I left four long scratches across his face. "I hate you! Mom, Dad are you just going to stand there and do nothing as this rapist tears our family apart? After I kicked him in his groin, my parents jumped in and began to help him. My mother grabbed me by my arms as my father pulled me to the ground. "What are you doing?" I screamed, "You should be helping me, he's the criminal not me, what are you doing? ..."

I woke up in a cold sweat. It was just another bad dream. With the force of fifteen years worth of pain and hurt I began to vomit. Year after year I endured one hellish nightmare after another, it had to stop. The only way to get over a trauma is to face it head on. It was time to face the dragon!

The dragon's long tail had not pasted over my older sister Sheree, she to was one of his victims. She also knew that it was time to confront him, she had also suffered from years of tormenting nightmares. Over and over again she re-lived the horror that he put her through. This man had plowed through our whole family and it was time for him to face the music.

For months we prayed and fasted until we heard from heaven, without a doubt we needed total guidance from the Lord. This delicate situation needed to be handled with the anointing, not with the flesh. We asked the Lord to help us with every detail, right down to the time, date, and place. Each time my sister and I spoke about the meeting, the both of us would literally get sick to our stomachs. It was one of the hardest things that we ever had to do. However, in order to maximize our God given potential we knew it was a must.

The purpose of the meeting was to make all concerning parties aware of the truth and to tell the real story so that even the dragon's wife would no longer be in the dark. I believe deep down inside she may have already known the truth, or if not the whole truth, she had to have known that something wasn't right.

The meeting would give everyone, including my parents, and even the dragon, an opportunity to free themselves from years of guilt, shame and pain.

8

DAY OF REDEMPTION

It would be hard for anyone to forget the sad day that Princes Diana, Queen of Hearts, was killed in a tragic car accident. Her life came to an untimely and tragic ending while racing away from the paparazzi in a Paris tunnel. Sadness fell upon the entire earth as the whole world mourned the death of a Princess.

It was a beautiful sunny Sunday morning. In spite of the world's sadness, I found joy in the fact that I was sitting next to my sister Sheree in church.

The preacher's white robe was decorated with beautiful stained glass colors that came through the window with the morning sun. Even though the word came forth with great power, it was difficult for me to concentrate on the message. I had one thing on my mind and that was what laid ahead for me and my sister later that afternoon.

Today was the big day, the day of the meeting. The night before we prayerfully prepared our parents. We informed them of our intentions so that there would be no misunderstandings and no surprises. The only one who would be surprised was the dragon and that's just how we wanted it.

It was four o'clock and the time was at hand. Sheree and I held each other's hands and took deep breaths as we gathered our thoughts. The tension was so thick that you could cut it with a knife. I watched as our mother discreetly faded into the background. She had become mysteriously quiet, perhaps she didn't want to wake up any skeletons in her closet.

Finally our father made the call. "Hey, how's everything? That's good, that's good. Say, ah, do you have a minute? I need you to come over here for a second. Great see ya in a few."

In less than five minutes we all heard the knock at the door, "up jumps the devil." He walks in to find my mother, Sheree, Sheree's prayer partner, my father, and myself. One look at me and he knew that something was very wrong.

The first thing he did was walk over to my sister and try to hug her. As she rejected his hug she asked him to have a seat. At this point he began to panic and sweat, his skin turned a horrible hue of ashy, dead man's gray. Time had not been kind to him, or should I say, sin had not been kind to him. His face looked like five miles of bad road on a stormy night. His body was reminiscent of a walking Q-tip that had been set on fire, then blown out by the winds of evil. Father time had given him a left hook and Mother Nature hadn't given him much time to recover.

My sister began to tell him the reason why we had called him over. He interrupted her by saying, "I can't discuss any of this because my wife isn't here, something like this ... we should both be here." He actually thought that we would let him off the hook because his wife wasn't there. She had been a part of the plan from the very beginning. Immediately I replied, "No problem, I'll get the phone." His jaw dropped as if it was going to hit the sofa. He really didn't think we would let him call her over. I handed him the phone, his hands were shaking like a jackhammer. He was so bewildered that he couldn't even dial his own phone number. He began to mumble as he spoke to my father. "I don't have my glasses, will you dial the number for me?" Sarcastically I replied, "Please, let me dial the number for you." After dialing the number I handed the phone too my father. Dad asked his wife to come over. In a few short minutes she to had joined us for the meeting.

Sheree greeted his wife, "Well, I wish we were coming together under better circumstances, however, ... Sheree went on to tell her about all of the childhood abuse that she suffered at the hands of her husband. The look on the dragon's wife's face was one of great humiliation and embarrassment. She never said that she did or did not believe my sister but everyone could plainly see that she believed every word.

My sister elaborated on the years of sexual misconduct that he had perpetrated against her. The reality of his sickness became more and more apparent with each passing moment. As my sister spoke, the dragon held his head up and asked her a question. "Do you feel that I took advantage of you?" The first thing that came to my mind was (we've gotta live one here!). Only a very sick and demented person could question the fact that an adult having full-blown sex with a child was an unfair advantage.

Soon it was my turn. I began to tell what had happened to me. I also stood proxy on behalf of the other three family members who were victimized. Of course he denied all charges. In essence he was calling me a liar. He began to get loud and rude and he actually began to accuse me of offending him. To add insult to injury, my parents sat right there and watching as this man insulted and discredited me and never said a word in my defense. I couldn't believe that my parents could allow this man to come into their home, admit to raping one daughter and allow him to speak to the other one like a dog! Unbelievable! It felt as if someone took a dull, jagged knife and ripped a ten-mile valley down the center of my heart and soul.

As I sat there and watched my parents say nothing on my behalf, I remembered the Word of God. Psalm 27:10 "When my father and mother forsake me, then the Lord will take me up."

I looked the dragon straight in the eyes and I stopped speaking to him and began to speak to the demons that occupied his entire existence. In a loud voice I called them out by their names; "Spirit of phedophilia, lying demon, spirit of manipulation, spirit of perversion, spirit of lying!" Once I addressed the spirits I silenced them in the name of Jesus! A gurgle choking sound began to come from his throat, the power of God shut his lying mouth right on the spot.

He had lied to his wife for so long that she didn't know what to believe. She began to cross-examine me as if I was to blame. Some times people don't want to know the truth since the truth hurts, it's always easier to play the blame game.

After we ended the meeting with prayer, I told the dragon that I believed that he would not close his eyes and leave this earth until he admitted what he had done to me and my other family members.

As for my mother, she was as quiet as a church mouse during the whole meeting. The only time she uttered a sound was when she interrupted me in order to defended the dragon. She asked me not to talk about our other sisters that he raped because it had nothing to do with the meeting. God knows it had everything to do with the meeting, that was the whole point.

The nightmares that I had for all those years had finally come true. As far as I was concerned my parents had sided with the dragon. If I had an ounce of respect left for my parents I had lost all of it on that day.

Two days later my parents went for a short drive outside of town, while out on the highway they got a flat tire. Who did they call to rescue them? None other than their very best friend the dragon. Immediately my parents resumed their relationship with him as if nothing had happened.

I believe in forgiveness, as is a must according to the word of God. However, there is a major difference between forgiveness and flat-out stupidity.

9

FOURTEEN DAYS OF DARKNESS

The moment that the meeting was adjourned, I fell into a very deep depression that lasted for fourteen days. The next day I arrived at work in a total trance. I could hear my co-workers as they talked to me but I literally could not talk back.

I couldn't believe what had happened, I was not at all pleased with how things had ended the day before. I now had to deal with what was and not with what I wished could be. I felt as if the day of redemption had laughed in my face, I couldn't understand why I kept ending up with the short end of the stick. Where was my justice, where was my shoulder to cry on? My mother had my father to lean on, my sister had her husband, and even the dragon had his wife. As for me, I had no one to comfort me, no one to say, "Hold on, everything's gonna be all right."

I had fallen into such a deep depression that I didn't want to see or talk to anyone. I just wanted to stay in the bed under the covers and hide from the whole world. suddenly I began to feel so filthy and dirty. A thousand showers could never wash away the feeling of dirtiness. I wanted to disappear, not die, not live, no soul, no spirit, just disappear.

The devil started to play games with my mind. He tried to convince me that my parents may have had something to do with all of this after all. Maybe they were all in on it together. Maybe they're all sex freaks, "swingers." I'd heard about these types of couples on talk shows. Maybe my father did tell him it was okay to have sex with his children. My mind was going a mile a minute, non-stop for fourteen days straight. I was in such pain and torment that my body produced a negative energy that could be felt long after I had left a room.

One morning while I sat under the covers in a dark state of depression, the Lord spoke to my heart. He told me that things aren't always how they seem. Although my parents seemed okay they too were dealing with a lot of pain and hurt. The Lord reminded me that He was God all by Himself, and He didn't want me to grieve over how He handles His business. "THE BATTLE IS NOT YOURS, IT IS MINE, and I will vindicate you. Take your eyes off of the situation and put them on Me. Walk by faith and not by sight." The Lord showed me how he had everything under control.

It was at that moment that I regained my freedom. God cleared my mind, my spirit and my heart. I was a free woman and I was glad about it. The Lord continued to minister to my soul as He reminded me that He was the source of my strength and happiness. As this complete turn around began to happen, the Lord engraved this scripture into my spirit, Romans 5:19 "For as by one man's disobedience many were made sinners, so by one man's obedience many will be made righteous."

The devil meant all of my life's trials for bad, but God meant it for my good. The Lord let me know that not one tear that fell from my eyes would be in vain. He assured me that with perseverance and obedience, many would be made righteous by the words of my testimony.

10

THERE'S A STRANGER IN TOWN

It was a beautiful sunny summer morning. I laid in bed a few extra minutes just to watch the fluffy white clouds pass by. The cool summer breeze that swept across my face through the bedroom window almost caressed me back to sleep. But I couldn't go back to sleep because I had to get to work on time.

After my morning regiment I was out of the door and into my little brown station wagon. First stop the corner store, I had to have my morning Java. As the store attendant filled my large cup with French vanilla coffee, I couldn't help but notice something strange about this day. It was a day like no other and I felt different as if something was about to happen, something life changing.

After paying for my coffee, I jumped back into my car and headed for work. As I waited to proceed into traffic, I kept feeling this strange pull to go the opposite direction. I remember thinking, "What is this feeling? ... I couldn't shake it. I have to call into work, I can't go to work today. I've never missed a day since I started this job so I'm sure they'll understand."

As I pulled my car back into the parking lot, I tried to understand the feeling that had come over me. While sitting there the Lord began to speak to me. He reminded me that it was Holy Convocation week at my church. Services were being held for seven days straight, including one which was to be held that afternoon. At that point I knew what the Lord was trying to tell me. I was supposed to be at church for the afternoon service.

Being obedient to the spirit of the Lord, I found myself in church later that day. Since I missed a full day of work, I thought I should make myself useful and help with the video ministry. As I set up the cameras I couldn't help but wonder what would today's message be about. I didn't even know who was speaking. I only knew that there was a stranger who was coming to town to give a seminar that afternoon and a service later that night.

As the service began the pastor stood to introduce the guest speaker. After a very lengthy and quite impressive introduction the preacher came forth. As she walked down the aisle I couldn't help but notice how Holy she looked. There was something different about this preacher, she wore no make-up and she didn't even have on any earrings. Her white suit seemed to hi-light her silver and black hair that was swirled into a french roll. She was not only an Evangelist, but an author and a demonology teacher as well. Some how I knew this evangelist had something important to say.

From the moment that she began to speak, I was in total awe. Finally, someone had the answer to all of my problems and my spirit bore witness to everything this woman of God spoke. I knew beyond a shadow of a doubt that she was telling the truth. She walked through the word of God with such authority, she was like a walking Bible.

As she proceeded to minister, she explained why the people of God struggled year after year with the same problems and why so many fall to the wayside. One scripture after another rolled off of her tongue like rivers of living water. She spoke with such fervency as she quoted Ephesians 6:12 "For we wrestle not against flesh and blood but against principalities, against powers, against the rulers of the darkness of this world, against spiritual wickedness in high places."

How could anyone remember all of those scriptures I wondered. She must have them written down some place, but I didn't see any papers. I guessed she had to know all of those scriptures because this woman was an exorcist, and I knew instinctively that she was truly anointed by God. She gave a complete break down of how demons enter into a person's body, their demonic groupings and how to get the spirits out once they have entered. I thought, "I have to get this ladies book, "Out of me went 43 demons." She's so tiny, how could 43 demons even fit inside of her? I leaned over and whispered to the person sitting next to me, "What's this ladies name again?" She said, "Evangelist Antoinette Cannaday."

After Evangelist Cannaday finished ministering to us, she held a prayer line. As she laid hands, people began to fly every where and you could even feel the anointing as she walked by.

Because I was video taping the service, I didn't get on the prayer line that afternoon, but I knew she was coming back that night. Deep down inside I knew that a very special blessing awaited me on the prayer line and I wasn't going to miss it for anything in the world.

Seven o' clock couldn't come around fast enough, even after it did, I began to get upset because it seemed like the church was singing too long.

All I wanted was the Word and that prayer line.

Finally Evangelist Cannaday stood to preach. She humbly approached the microphone with all of that Holy Ghost power leading the way. In the midst of her anointing, she never forgot to pay homage to her pastor, Bishop Roy Bryant Sr., D.D. She gave great reverence and respect to the man of God who cast the forty-three demons from her body."

Soon she began to preach, Just from the word of God alone the church was rocked to their feet. The power of God swept across the congregation like a mighty whirlwind. At last she spoke the words that I had waited to hear all day long, "It's prayer time." The prayer line stretched from one end of the church to the other, and back around again. I couldn't believe she was going to pray for all of those people, but she did. As she prayed, people began to fall all over the place, over the seats, under the seats up and down the aisle.

With the help of a very well trained entourage, The Vessels Unto Honor Deliverance Ministries, she moved through the prayer line with the greatest of ease. She was accompanied by approximately thirteen well-dressed and highly anointed women. Her group worked together like a well-oiled Holy Ghost machine. Although this group consisted of many people, they worked together as if they were one person. Finally it was my turn for prayer, I held my hands up high with out stretched arms lifted towards heaven. When she laid hands on me it felt like I had been hit with lightning. I had never felt the power of God like that before in my life. I was out like a light. I had no idea that at that very moment, the Lord had birthed me into my destiny.

After the Holy Convocation week, I became more eager to learn than ever. I had been exposed to life changing information through the ministry of Evangelist Cannaday, and I was never the same again.

The lesbian lifestyle that I once lead was far from me and I had grown to be rooted, grounded and steadfast in the Lord. Though my only desire was to be more like Jesus, I still had struggles and issues that I needed to address. Beyond a shadow of a doubt, I knew that I needed deliverance. The word deliverance is used so casually in the church world that it has lost it's true meaning and most people don't really know what true deliverance is all about.

I knew that at all cost, I had to get in touch with Evangelist Cannaday. She had the answers, she knew the truth and she preached about things that most pastors refuse to admit exist. This woman of God knew that Christians could have a demon, and she had the anointing to do something about it. I studied the literature and listened to all of the tapes that she bought with her when she came to our church. Most of the tapes had the voice of her pastor Bishop Roy Bryant Sr., D.D. on them. I recalled thinking, "If Evangelist Cannaday is as knowledgeable and as anointed as she is, how much more knowledgeable and anointed must her bishop be. Without a doubt he must be a great man of God. I wonder what he looks like, how old is he? Judging by the sound of his voice, he must be a great big man, with a whole lot of confidence in God."

Day after day I listened to the tapes, wanting so desperately to have Evangelist Cannaday work with me in deliverance. So many times I wanted to call her, but I always thought she would be to busy to talk to me. Finally there came a day that I mustered up enough courage to give her a call.

To my surprise she was as nice over the phone as she was in person, she told me to call her any time I wanted to. She even set a date for me to come in for a private deliverance session.

11

DELIVERANCE HAS COME

"I've always loved train rides, that's why I decided to take the train today. The Hudson line is the most beautiful view I've ever seen. The silver water proudly reflects the beautiful rolling mountains along the riverside. One moment you're in the heart of one of the biggest cities in the world, the next minute you're in the most beautiful countryside imaginable."

It wasn't very cold on the train that day, but I couldn't stop shivering. Maybe it was because I was on the way to my first deliverance session. As my hands trembled, I looked down at the small piece of paper that I held. On it were written the directions that Evangelist Cannaday had given me over the phone. It seemed as if I read the directions a hundred times. Nervously I squirmed around in my seat, without a doubt, I was scared. I had never seen a private deliverance before, so I didn't know what to expect.

"Yonkers, this stop Yonkers." Finally the conductor announced my stop. It seemed as if the ride was just a little bit longer that day. After hopping two buses and walking three blocks I was finally there. As I walked up the stone Staircase, I looked up at the clock in the center of the steeple. I couldn't help but marvel at the beautiful architecture of the church. (But a holiness church inside of a cathedral?), I couldn't believe it.

As I walked inside, I was greeted with the most beautiful stained glass windows that I had ever seen. I looked up at the bi-level ceilings, they were at least twenty-five feet high. My eyes followed the ruby red carpet down the center aisle, right into the pulpit, which was encased by a beautiful altar.

Evangelist Cannaday met me in the outer vestibule. Right away she could see that I was very nervous. After greeting me, she addressed my nervousness. Evangelist Cannaday began to explain, "Nervousness is very common, however, it's not you that is doing all of that trembling, it's the demons. They know that they have but a short time and they are scared. They know that they have to come out." At her words, my body began to tremble even the more.

As she led me to her office, she told me that she wanted me to meet someone. "This is my deliverance partner, Evangelist Mary Garland. We have been in the ministry together for over seventeen years and she will be working with me today. Have a seat in this chair." She sat me in a chair in the middle of the room. With a funny little grin on her face she told me that it was the hot seat. She handed me a stack of paper towels while sitting a small trash can next to my chair. Evangelist Cannaday stood to my left while Evangelist Garland stood to my right as it was time to get started. Evangelist Cannaday told me that they we're going to have me renounce some things, she said "Repeat after me ..." She had me renounce every demonic thing that I had ever been involved in, including lesbianism. I couldn't understand why she would have me renounce lesbianism, I wasn't gay. I wasn't involved in that sort of thing any more.

She then said, "Okay Rettie were going to start to work now. If you feel anything come up, it's okay, that's what the napkins are for. Don't swallow any thing, let it come out."

She and Evangelist Garland began to pray, as they prayed she put her hand on my forehead. Her hands felt burning hot, as if it would leave a scar. She began to call out different spirits, (ANGER, REJECTION, ASTHMA, UNFORGIVENESS, CORRUPT COMMUNICATION), as she did my body began to react, I began to shake and quiver. Loud and strange voices began to come out of my mouth. Bad turned to worse the moment she called out the spirit of lesbianism. A loud scream came up from my throat, and out of my mouth, the spirit of lesbianism began to speak. "I'm not coming out of here, this is my home. Do you know how long I've been in here? For years. I'm running things! I wear the pants.

No one is going to tell me what to do. I'm her personality. Rettie needs me, I'm her friend. We use to party and we picked up women together. She would be lost without me, I'm her personality!!! Who do you think you are Cannaday? You can't get me out of here. I was doing just fine until Rettie started going to church, now I can't work. Now she's listening to you, you're gonna ruin everything Cannaday, stop talking to her, leave her alone Cannaday, you don't know what your doing, you're in way over your head this time."

Evangelist Cannaday emphatically replied, "Rettie doesn't want you, she's already renounced you. Stop

79

talking and come out, I'm going to burn you if you don't come out; okay 1,2,3, out!" I heard the spirit shout, "Okay, Okay, I'm out!" Evangelist Cannaday replied, "If you're out, why are you still talking? Come out and bring your nest up with you." "We can't come out, the voice whimpered, we have to stop her, we can't come out, if we come out she'll tell on us, she has a big mouth just like you Cannaday. She's gonna expose us, she's gone far enough, we have to stop her. She'll tell on us and others will be set free, we'll loose our homes. You're no match for us Cannaday, we'll bring you down if we have to. Leave us alone!!"

Evangelist Cannaday began to launch attacks on other supporting spirits, "Jezebel, come out in the name of Jesus" suddenly a loud scream came out of my mouth. The spirit of Jezebel began to speak, "Who told you I was in here? I'm not coming out of here, no ones gonna tell me what to do. We wear the pants, no ones gonna tell me what to do. I hate men and I hate you Cannaday. We're gonna destroy Rettie, she has a big mouth, were gonna kill her!"

After working for over an hour the two evangelist had cast out more demons than I could count, I was loaded. A born again Holy Spirit filled Christian, and I had demons! After hearing the demons speak, it was at that moment that I realized who "justification" was. Justification was the spirit of Jezebel! She is a man hating demon, she works very closely with the spirit of lesbianism and rebellion. Instantly everything had become so clear to me. All those years demons had been talking to me, trying to destroy me. For so long I thought that those nasty, filthy thoughts were my own. Those thoughts didn't belong to me, they belonged to Satan and that's just who I gave them back to.

Just when I thought it was all over, Evangelist Cannaday began to call out lesbianism again, "Lesbianism, come out in the name of Jesus!" Before I knew what had happened to me, the lesbian spirit threw my body down to the floor. I was rolling around as the spirit screamed and hollered. "No, No, please, don't make me leave, my work is not done here. I have to destroy Rettie ... Noooooo!" With the force of ten men, my hands grabbed my new shirt in the collar area. As the demon of lesbianism began to come out of my body, my hands ripped my shirt straight down the middle! At that moment the screaming stopped. The un-clean spirit had left my body and I was free! Praise the Lord!

Fortunately I had finally received the deliverance that I so desperately needed. I was tired, but I felt good inside, I was as free as a bird, or so I thought.

Evangelist Cannaday enlightened me by saying, "Rettie, you received some great deliverance, but you'll be needing more. We'll have to set you another appointment within the next two weeks. You'll need to monitor yourself over the next few days. Just let me know how you're feeling so we'll know what to look for next time. Rettie, how are you feeling?" I answered, "I didn't know that I had so many demons. As for lesbianism, how could that demon have possibly been inside of me. I'm not gay any more, I haven't even had a gay thought in eons. Without hesitation, she quickly explained, "Rettie, for years you were involved in a lot of perverse things, it took time to get in the state that you were in, and it's going to take some time to get out. As for the spirit of lesbianism, demons can lie dormant for a season or even for years. Though you may not have gay feelings, or the personal desire to be involved with like activities, that doesn't mean that the demon was dislodged. This is a very common misconception. Remember, Satan is patient, he doesn't mind waiting for the perfect opportunity to activate a demon who has been lying dormant. That's why year after year saints keep finding themselves in the same old traps. For true deliverance a demonic spirit must be cast out of the human body.

The next morning I awoke giving God great glory, I felt so good inside. After my morning prayer, I called Evangelist Cannaday to thank her once more, and to let her know how great I felt. Her level of anointing was so high, that even during that phone conversation I began to get more deliverance. I couldn't believe it, demons actually recognize the voices of those who have authority over them. (Jesus I know, Paul I know; but who are ye? *Acts 19:15-16*)

After hearing the unadulterated word of God and witnessing the signs and wonders that followed, I knew that it was time to seek God on a whole new level. Shortly after my first deliverance session, I was led by the Lord to leave my church and join The Bible Church Of Christ Inc. under the leadership of Bishop Roy Bryant Sr., D.D.

My deliverance continued for many months, it was sad to see just how much damage Satan had really done to me. Most people would be amazed to know just how many demonic spirits a human body can actually hold. I was delivered from spirits that I didn't even know existed, such as the spirit of masculinity. The spirit of masculinity is a "man spirit." It causes women to dress and act like a man. This spirit is most commonly found in lesbian women who play the "butch role" or the aggressor. The spirit of masculinity was cast out of my body by my pastor, Bishop Bryant Sr. I had called him for a reason that was totally unrelated to my deliverance. During our phone conversation a deep male's voice began to come out of my mouth. Bishop Roy Bryant Sr. began to question the spirit, "What is your name?" I heard the deep voice speaking out of my mouth say, "My name is masculinity." Bishop Bryant Sr. began to address the demon. "You have to come out of her, Rettie is a woman of God now, you have no right to be there." The demon answered "I have rights, I'm a man, in fact, I'm more of a man than you are Roy!"

Bishop Bryant Sr. replied, "Okay, we'll see just how much of a man you are when I cast you out!"

The next day Bishop Bryant met with me in his office for private deliverance. Within five minutes he had cast the male spirit from my body. Bishop Roy Bryant Sr. explained to me that the spirits of masculinity, lesbianism, jezebel, hatred for men, rape and molestation were called groupings. These spirits travel together impregnating innocent people usually during childhood years.

I asked him why did I feel so lost after each deliverance session, as if my identity was missing. He answered, "Because you don't know who you are! For many years these spirits were thinking for you, telling you what to do, what to wear and even where to go. They had become your personality. Now that you've been delivered, you must learn to think for yourself and develop your own personality. Due to the sexual and emotional trauma that you endured as a child, Satan crept in and stole your womanhood. Now that you have become the woman that God intended you to be, you have to take time to get to know the "true you." It's going to take some time, but you'll be just fine"

12

WHAT DOES GOD SAY
ABOUT HOMOSEXUALITY?

In the book of Romans the Lord clearly speaks to us concerning homosexuality. Through the Apostle Paul, He lets us know exactly how he feels about lesbianism and other acts of wickedness. Romans 1:21-32 "Because that, when they knew God, they glorified him not as God, neither were thankful; but became vain in their imaginations, and their foolish heart was darkened. 22. Professing themselves to be wise, they became fools, 23. And changed the glory of the incorruptible God into an image made like to corruptible man, and to birds, and four-footed beasts, and creeping things. 24. Wherefore God also gave them up to uncleanness through the lust of their own hearts, to dishonor their own bodies between themselves: 25. Who changed the truth of God into a lie, and worshipped and served the creature more than the Creator, who is blessed forever. Amen.

26. For this cause God gave them up unto vile affections: for even their women did change the natural use into that which is against nature: (i.e. Lesbianism, oral sex, and sex paraphernalia)

27. And likewise also the men, leaving the natural use of the woman, burned in their lust one toward another; men with men working that which is unseemly, and receiving in themselves that recom-

pense of their error which was meet. (i.e. homosexuals, oral sex & sodomites)

28. And even as they did not like to retain God in their knowledge, God gave them over to a reprobate mind, to do those things which are not convenient; 29. Being filled with all unrighteousness, fornication, wickedness, covetousness, maliciousness; full of envy, murder, debate, deceit, malignity; whisperers, 30. Backbiters, haters of God, despiteful, proud, boasters, inventors of evil things, (i.e. pornography/sex paraphernalia) disobedient to parents, 31. Without understanding, covenant breakers, without natural affection, implacable, unmerciful: 32. Who knowing the judgment of God, that they which commit such things are worthy of death, not only do the same, but have pleasure in them that do them."

After reading Romans 1:21-32 there is no question as to how strongly God disapproves of homosexuality. God hates this sin! The Lord goes on to tell us in the book of Corinthians that we will be held accountable for the deeds that we performed with our bodies. 2 Corinthians 5:10 "For we must all appear before the judgement seat of Christ; that every one may receive the things done in his body, according to that he hath done, whether it be good or bad. 11. Knowing therefore the terror of the Lord, we persuade men; but we are made manifest unto God; and I trust also are made manifest in our consciences."

There is no way around God's word, in the book of Matthew 24:35, Jesus said "Heaven and earth will pass away, but My word will by no means pass away." Lining up with God's word cuts strongly against the sinful nature of man. Being born into sin and shaped by iniquity (Psalms 51:5) living Holy is an unnatural state for man. That is why we must die daily of the flesh, (1 Corin. 15: 31) in order to maintain righteousness before God. It is only through our Comforter, the Holy Spirit, that we are able to do so.

The fact that homosexuality is also fornication is often over looked. Throughout the Bible the Lord has emphasized his great dislike for fornicators, as stated once again in the book of Corinthians. 1 Corin. 6:9-10 "Know ye not that the unrighteous shall not inherit the kingdom of God? Be not deceived: neither fornicators, nor idolaters, nor adulterers, nor effeminate (homosexual), nor abusers of themselves with mankind, 10. Nor thieves, nor covetous nor drunkards, nor revilers, nor extortioners, shall inherit the kingdom of God."

Overcoming the flesh is one of the hardest task for mankind to accomplish. However, through the Holy Spirit the Lord has given us the ability to walk holy and circumspectly before Him. The Apostle Paul tells us in the book of Romans, that it is our reasonable service to be a living sacrifice. (Romans 12:1-2 "I beseech you therefore, brethren, by the mercies of God, that ye present your bodies a living sacrifice, holy, acceptable unto God, which is your reasonable service. 2. And be not conformed to this world: but be ye transformed by the renewing of your mind, that ye may prove what is that good and acceptable, and perfect, will of God.") What is a living sacrifice? In essence it is to die yet live, to die of oneself and ones own will and desires. The Apostle Paul tells us that it is our reasonable service to die of our flesh for if we do not, it is impossible to do the perfect will of God. Dying of the flesh evolves with the renewing of the mind. Philippines 2:5 "Let this mind be in you, which was also in Christ Jesus:"

Throughout the Bible the Lord shows us time and time again that He is not pleased with homosexuality and lesbian activities. Who can forget how God destroyed two whole cities for that very cause? The cities of Sodom and Gomorrah were filled with great promiscuity and Sodomy. The Lord was grieved because their sins were great, (Gen. 18:20).

The Bible says that in the heat of the day three angels appeared unto Abraham. The angels did not hide from Abraham that the twin cities of Sodom and Gomorrah would be destroyed because of their wickedness. After the angels prophesied to Abraham and Sarah concerning the birth of their son, the angels turned their faces towards Sodom and went their way (Gen. 18:21).

But Abraham stood yet before the Lord and pleaded on behalf of the cities so that God would not destroy them. Gen. 18:25-26 "That be far from thee to do after this manner, to slay the righteous with the wicked: and that the righteous should be as the wicked, that be far from thee: Shall not the judge of all the earth do right? 26. And the Lord said, If I find in Sodom fifty righteous within the city, then I will spare all the placed for their sakes."

For the love of souls, Abraham asked God on a peradventure basis to pull the count of the righteous down to only ten. (Gen. 18:32) "And he said, Oh let not the Lord be angry, and I will speak yet but this once: Peradventure ten shall be found there. And He said, I will not destroy it for ten's sake."

The Word of God goes on to tell us that the two angels who went to Sodom were greeted by Lot, who was Abraham's nephew. Lot invited the two men to stay at his house for a feast, and they did bake unleavened bread and ate. Gen. 19:4-5 "But before they lay down, the men of the city, even the men of Sodom, compassed the house round, both old and young, all the people from every quarter: 5. And they called unto Lot, and said unto him, Where are the men which came in to thee this night? bring them out unto us, that we may know them. (have sexual relations with them.)

But Lot pleaded with them not to do such a wicked thing and offered the men his daughters, who were virgins instead of the angels. But the men of Sodom did not want his daughters, they wanted to lay with the men who were in his house. The crowed warned Lot that if he did not let them in, they would do even worse to him than they had planned to do to the men inside.

Gen. 19:10-11 "But the men (the angels) put forth their hand, and pulled Lot into the house to them, and shut to the door. 11. And they smote the men that were at the door of the house with blindness, both small and great: so that they wearied themselves to find the door." The angels told Lot to get his family together and leave the city because the Lord had sent them there to destroy it.

Gen. 19:27-29 "And Abraham got up early in the morning to the place where he stood before the Lord: 28. And he looked toward Sodom and Gomorrah, and toward all the land of the plain, and beheld, and, lo, the smoke of the country went up as the smoke of a furnace. 29. And it came to pass, when God destroyed the cities of the plain, that God remembered Abraham, and sent Lot out of the midst of the overthrow, when he overthrew the cities in which Lot dwelt."

The spirit of homosexuality is a strong spirit! This spirit had overtaken two whole cities, so much so that not even ten righteous people were found within. The spirit of sodomy had driven the men of the city into a state of frenzy. The angels had to blind the Sodomites eyes to keep themselves safe from the demons of lust and sodomy which possessed them.

In today's modern world, there are cities within the souls of men that have been overtaken by homosexuality, but God is yet a deliverer. 1 Chronicles 16:34 "O give thanks unto the Lord; for He is good; for His mercy endureth for ever." The Word tells us that God's will is that not any should perish, but that all should come to repentance (2 Peter 3:9). Because God is no respecter of persons, there is no good thing that He will withhold from those who diligently seek Him, this includes deliverance. Deliverance is an equal opportunity solution for homosexuals, lesbians and all who are bound and oppressed by Satan and his tactics. However, deliverance is a two way street. There are many people who want deliverance and or healing only to end the torment that the demons are perpetrating upon them. All to often people want the attributes of God and not God Himself. They don't want a relationship with Jesus, they don't want to change their lifestyle, and they don't want to be filled with the Holy Spirit. Such people are not candidates for deliverance. In the book of Matthew 12:43-45 Jesus tells us that "When the unclean spirit is gone out of a man, he (the unclean spirit) walketh through dry places, seeking rest and findeth none. 44. Then he saith, I will return into my house (meaning the person) from whence I came out; and when he is come, he findeth it empty (no Holy Spirit), swept, and garnished. 45. Then goeth he, and taketh with himself seven other spirits more wicked than himself, and they enter in and dwell there: and the last state of that man is worse than the first. Even so shall it be also unto this wicked generation."

However, there are millions of men and women who are candidates for deliverance, who truly want to live according to God's perfect word. Like Hannah who cried out to God in her despair, the Lord will answer those who call upon His name, and no good thing will He withhold from them.

In a world that is filled with imperfections, it is great to know that there is a perfect God who will supply all of our needs, according to His riches in glory.

13

SHAKING THE STIGMA: LIVING HOLY AND FREE

Let's face it, there is a stigma that lingers over the heads of those who have been delivered from the spirit of homosexuality or lesbianism. It's that little unspoken "thing" that just won't go away, that very "thing" that almost becomes a personal trade mark; "Oh, you mean the lady that used to be gay?" This type of treatment can be tough for any saint, but what about the sinner? Surprisingly enough in today's "Out of the closet" society, there are some saints including pastors, who will not minister to homosexuals because they are homophobic. Phobias are fears. The Lord has not given us a spirit of fear, but of love, power and a sound mind.

In these last and evil days, there will be an overwhelming influx of homosexuals entering into the house of God. These souls will be looking to the church for answers and deliverance. How can the body of Christ help deliver souls from a spirit that has raped our nation, if we can not get past our own prejudices? Romans 3:23 reminds us that we have all fallen short of the glory of God.

Even within the house of God shaking the stigma can be a most difficult task. I myself have found that long after the Lord delivered me, there were still those who questioned my freedom. The bulk of the stigma that was attached to my life, was broken by the power of my testimony. Although every former gay or lesbian person is not called to go public with their testimony, testifying is still yet one of God's most powerful tools.

Satan works best in secrecy and in darkness. Even after deliverance he enjoys exposing our past in order to create new scandals. I found that through testifying, I dis-enpower the devil. I told everything about my past before he had a chance to. This left little or no leverage at all for him to work with.

It is important for me to emphasize the fact that I was anointed by God to give my testimony, and all glory and honor belongs to Jesus. With such a testimony, there comes much persecution, judgment, and long suffering. However, the Lord blessed me with a very strong anointing making me equal to the task. Had I not been hand picked and chosen by God for this type of ministry, I would have fallen by the wayside a long time ago.

Living holy reflects directly back to one's church home. It is virtually impossible to live holy without being taught under a Holiness ministry. "Holiness without which no man shall see the Lord"(Hebrews 12:14). True holiness has almost become a thing of the past, the same activities that are seen in the world are now seen in many of today's churches. Fewer preachers than ever are preaching emphatically against sin, most have become nothing more than motivational speakers.

True enough God's word is inspirational, but it is also a two edged sword, which cuts deep enough to reach the very marrow of man's soul.

The one true remedy for shaking the stigma and living holy and free is the anointing! The closer we get to Jesus the farther away we get from the opinions of man. Through our Comforter, the Holy Spirit, the Lord will surely give his Saints V.O.P., "Victory Over People."

14

CAN A PERSON BE BORN HOMOSEXUAL OR LESBIAN?

Can a person be born gay or lesbian? This has to be one of the oldest and most pondered questions of all times. When this question is asked it is most commonly asked from a scientific, social or humanistic viewpoint. However, homosexuality and lesbianism is not a scientific, social, or humanistic issue, as earlier stated it is a spiritual issue. It is a little known fact however, that a spiritual issue can have physical side affects. In the case of homosexuality the side effects will some times manifest itself as extreme feminine behavior which can lead to cross dressing or even transsexual surgeries. In some cases, lesbians will experience similar side effects, in which case the side effects will manifest itself as masculine behavior. It is important to remember that these side effects are also demons.

Yet the question still remains, can a person be born gay or lesbian? The answer is absolutely, positively YES! As for that tailgating question which will inevitably follow; "How can one be born this way?" Answering this question from a demonology standpoint is quite simple.

The average person would be shocked and surprised to discover just how many people have been involved (in some shape or form) in lesbianism or homosexual activities. In some cases (I would dare to say in most cases) these same people can be found within our families.

The word of God says that He would "visit(ing) the iniquity of the fathers upon the children, and upon the children's children, unto the third and to the fourth generation." (Ex 34:7) The Devil knows that life begins at the moment of conception, therefore he will assign generational curses and other demons to lie waiting in the womb of a woman or in the seed of a man. These spirits will some times lay dormant for years or even generations, patiently awaiting the moment to enter into an unborn child. The unborn child having inherited those spirits, will most likely act out the desires of the demons at some point in their lives.

Generational curses do not end with homosexuality and lesbianism, there are countless spirits that travel through the bloodline. Below is a list of just a few spirits that can be found within families.

*High blood pressure	*Obesity
*Perversion	*Stealing
*Sugar diabetes	*Poverty
*Incarceration	*Drug Addiction
*Teen pregnancy	*Asthma
*Spousal abuse	*Lying
*Incest	*Cancer
*Suicide	*Mental Illness
*Divorce	*Depression

15

FULL TIME IN THE MINISTRY

Shortly after my deliverance, I had to take time out to become acquainted with myself. No longer having demons to tell me what to do, learning to think for myself was step number one. I had to get to know my likes, dislikes and my true inner feelings. For so many years I had been someone else, someone different, far from the woman of God that I should have been.

I truly didn't know how to carry myself like a lady on any long term or constant basis. I didn't really know how to dress, walk, sit or talk like a lady, I was so rough around the edges that it was simply pathetic. But with a little help from my friends and a whole lot of help from the Holy Spirit, things began to turn around very quickly.

No longer contending with the spirit of masculinity, instantly my female instincts began to kick-in. Like any young lady I discovered what it was that I liked to do best, shop! Right away I found myself walking the streets of the city, shopping, getting my hair done, and buying a whole new wardrobe.

While on one of my little shopping sprees, I remember crossing the busy streets of Manhattan, as I held my head up I saw a very pretty lady walking towards me. Taking a closer look, I realized that lady was my own reflection in a store window. Within myself I yelled, "Wow, that's me? Look every body, I'm a lady, I'm a lady! Thank God for deliverance."

God began to do an awesome and quick work in my life. So much so that before I took my first suit to the cleaners, He had placed me full-time in the ministry as the Public Relations Agent for the Bible Church Of Christ Inc.

At the mass deliverance prayer breakfasts that my pastor Bishop Roy Bryant Sr. holds, he almost always calls upon me to testify. Through the power of my testimony, I had gone from complete obscurity to total notoriety within a worldwide ministry. As a reward for my boldness, the Lord continuously opens doors for me on both a natural and spiritual plain, far to awesome to describe.

How excellent is the God we serve, everything that the devil meant for bad, Jesus turned it around for good. Every pain, every hurt, every childhood trauma, Jesus is now using it to help set the captive free. Yet none of these great works could have been possible without deliverance.

Through the deliverance ministry of the Bible Church Of Christ Inc., I have been delivered from more than twenty-five demons; anger, hurt, bitterness, fear, panic attacks, junk food, extra strength, rejection, rebellion, lust, lesbianism, corrupt communication, domineering spirit, cursing, witchcraft, fornication, worldly music, hurt from molestation, pants spirit, seduction, murder, asthma, fear of death, and stubbornness, just to name a few.

I thank God for deliverance! I thank Him for taking me by my hand, leading me out of the gay bars and nightclubs and into his marvelous light. I thank God that he took men's clothing off of my back and replaced it with a rob of righteousness. I also thank him for anointing me to carry his precious gospel throughout the world. And mostly I thank him for filling me with his precious Holy Spirit!

16

LIST OF DEMONIC SPIRITS

The following is a list of various demons actually encountered in the mass deliverance services held by my pastor Bishop Roy Bryant Sr., D.D. This list can also be found on page 345 in his book "Manual On Demonology, Diary Of An Exorcist." These demonic spirits have controlled the lives of God's people as well as the people of the world, these spirits are not habits or just something troubling individuals, they are demons. However, everything is not a demon, but there is a demon for everything.

For example, chocolate is not demonic. However, if a person is eating six or seven candy bars before breakfast, then of course there's a problem. Anything that is contrary to the word of God, or anything that is uncontrollable *is* demonic.

adultery
can't give love
separation of family
perverseness
bisexuality
gay spirit
divorce
false marriage
(common law)
boyfriend spirit

drugs/substance abuse
cocaine
heroin
tranquilizers
sleeping pills
medications
antidepressants
caffeine
(soda/coffee/tea)
alcohol

girlfriend spirit
polygamy
Uncleanliness
homosexuality
effeminate
lesbianism
oral sex
masturbation
promiscuity
whore spirit
unloved
can't receive love
incest
self-seduction
loneliness
unwanted
fear
hopelessness
depression
suicide
loss of libido
(no sexual)
lust
barrenness
sterility
impotency
tube blockage
womb blockage
infection spirit
abortion spirit
insecurity

nicotine
marijuana
salt
sugar/sweets
chocolate
nervous tension
anger

rejection
self-rejection
cursing
corrupt communication
fighting
murder
temper
hatred
hostility
rage
wrath
allergy
hayfever

Junkfood demon
under-eating
overeating/gluttony
obesity
anxiety
resentment
can't receive sensitivity
bitterness
criticism

backsliding
hindrance from
reading God's word
false religion
religious demon
heresy
selfishness
complaining spirit
infirmity
curse inheritance
poverty
spirit of mother
spirit of father
unteachableness
self-accusation
guilt
shame
compulsive confession
faults confession
rock music demon
rap music
pain
throat infection
memory loss
tiredness
narcolepsy
confusion
backbiting
profanity
telephone demon
memory recall

weakness
mind blockage

laziness
judgmental spirit
animosity
pride
anemia
cancer
cysts/tumors/fibroids
tubule infections
female disorders
talkativeness
self-judgment
self-condemnation
unworthiness
defeat
forgetfulness
disco demon
dancing demon
ear blockage
ear infection
deafness
fatigue
slumber
procrastination
gossiping
lying
scandalizing
deception
unforgiveness

rebellion
stubbornness
murmuring
word blockage
religious error
importance
respect of persons
intolerance
impatience
jealousy
envy
possessiveness
covetousness
destruction
self-destruction
destroyer
domineering spirit
hatred of women
hatred of husband
hatred of parents
molestation
separation from family
headaches
stress
kleptomania
stealing
debt
dishonesty
daydreams
fornication
mental depression

self-hatred
defiance
T.V. spirit
soap opera spirit
intellectual spirit
arrogance
fear of public opinion
perfection spirit
contention
frustration
infirmity
deformity
arthritis
diabetes
aids
Jezebel
hatred of men
hatred of wife
hatred of pastor
abuse spirit
harlotry
hypertension
post traumatic stress
pressure from family
pressure from church
filthy lucre
greed
fantasy lust
vivid imagination
lust of the eyes
withdrawal

suicide
self-pity
discouragement
obsession
mockery
schizophrenia
false religion
fingernail biting
importance
psychic
horoscope
fear of death
rape spirit
fear of men/women

fear of parents
stupidity
worry
racist spirit
bulimia

hopelessness
despondency
insomnia
slothfulness
double mindedness
false prophet
hurts
abnormal strength
witchcraft
astrology
spirit of death
child molestation
fear of people
pac man spirit
(i.e., video games)
torment
pride
self-will
anorexia
sensitivity

Bible Church Of Christ Book Listings

"Manual On Demonology, Diary Of An Exorcist"
Bishop Roy Bryant Sr. D.D. Author

"Manual On Demonology #2 Satan The Motavater"
Bishop Roy Bryant Sr. D.D. Author

"Out Of Me Went 43 Demons"
Evangelist Antoinette Cannaday Author

"Silence Equals Death — Exposing The Deeds Of Darkness"
Rettie Winfield Author

THE BIBLE CHURCH OF CHRIST, INC.
BISHOP ROY BRYANT Sr. D.D.
FOUNDER AND PASTOR

The Bible Church Of Christ
Headquarters
1358 Morris Avenue,
Bronx, New York 10453
(718) 293-1928

The Bible Church Of Christ
100 West 2nd Street
(Corner of 8th Avenue)
Mount Vernon, N.Y. 10550
(914) 664-4062

The Bible Church Of Christ
ANNEX
1069 Morris Ave.,
(Corner of 166th Street)
Bronx, New York 10456
(718) 588-2284

The Bible Church Of Christ
DELAWARE
(In Diamond Acres)
Dagsboro, Delaware 19939
(302) 732-3351

THE BIBLE CHURCH OF CHRIST, INC.
THEOLOGICAL INSTITUTES
Dr. ROY BRYANT, Sr., - President

THEOLOGICAL INSTITUTE
BRONX,
358 Morris Avenue,
(Corner of 170th Street)
Bronx, New York 10456
(718) 588-2284

THEOLOGICAL INSTITUTE
100 West 2nd Street
(Corner of 8th Avenue)
Mount Vernon, New York
10550
(718) 664-4602

THEOLOGICAL INSTITUTE
(In Diamond Acres)
Dagsboro, Delaware 19939
(302) 732-3351

VARIOUS TAPES
BY BISHOP ROY BRYANT, Sr., D.D.

DEMONOLOGY

~ Demons Speaking Tape No. 1
~ Demons Speaking Tape No. 2
~ Demons Speaking Tape No. 3
~ Self Deliverance
~ Who's In Your Body With You? (6 Tapes)
~ Exposing The Enemy From Within-Demon
    Manifestation
    Satan The Motivator (2 Tapes)
~ Demons and their Activities (conversation with
    Bishop Roy Bryant Sr. D.D. and Evangelist
    Antoinette Cannaday)
~ A Minister In Distress
~ Expelling Demons From The Home
~ How To Cast Out Demon (2 Tapes)
~ Satan On The Loose (3 Tapes)
~ Deliverance Prayer Breakfasts

    Deliverance Teachings
    Power Of The Word and The Blood
    No. 3. Overcoming The Wiles Of The Devil
    No 4. Oppression or Possession?
    The Works and Nature of Demons

Scriptures on Demons and Witchcraft
Demons Grouping

SEMINARS

Heresies
The Holy Spirit (4 Tapes)
What Makes a Carnal Church
The Gifts
Marriage and Sexuality
The Ministry of Jesus Christ (St. Matthew 10)
The Ministry of Jesus Christ - Part II
Tapes from The Ministers' Training Class
Relationships In The Churches
Was Adam Saved? (2 Tapes)

You may order tapes and book from:
The Bible Church Of Christ Christian Bookstore
1358 Morris Avenue
Bronx, New York 10456

Each Tape is $6.50. Add $1.50 for
postage and handling

<u>VIDEO TAPES</u>
Video tapes are also available
such as:
THE LAYING ON OF HANDS
(*How To Release The Anointing*)
By Bishop Roy Bryant Sr. D.D

GOLD TRIED IN THE FIRE
By Evangelist Cannaday
AND
SAVED AND ON THE WAY TO HELL
By Evangelist Antoinette Cannaday

And much, much more!
Call The Bible Church Of Christ Mt. Vernon
location for order forms and/or to place phone
orders. (914) 664-4602